Rules for
Descriptive Cataloging

in the Library of Congress

(Adopted by the American Library Association)

U. S.

~~THE~~ LIBRARY OF CONGRESS

DESCRIPTIVE CATALOGING DIVISION

WASHINGTON 1949

THE LIBRARY OF CONGRESS
PHOTODUPLICATION SERVICE
WASHINGTON 25, D. C.

catalog cards, is often a deciding factor in the adoption of certain rules; other libraries using the rules will have to decide for themselves at what point they wish to depart from them. To achieve uniformity which will expedite cooperative cataloging and international bibliography it is essential that a single set of rules be established. Cataloging for purely local uses need not conform if local needs do not require conformity. For instance, a library with a small collection of music may not use any form of conventional title or may well use a simpler form than that provided by these rules.

Two new chapters have been added: the rules for cataloging different issues of a given work if they are to be distinguished in the catalog, and the rules for cataloging incunabula. The latter chapter is based very closely on the section on incunabula which appeared in the *A. L. A. Catalog Rules* (preliminary American 2d ed. Chicago, American Library Association, 1941).

Rules are still lacking for the cataloging of several types of materials: sound recordings, motion pictures, manuscripts, prints and photographs, and books for the blind. The Library of Congress has not begun the printing of cards for these materials and rules are still to be developed.

It would be ungrateful not to acknowledge the help of the section heads in the Descriptive Cataloging Division who contributed very generously to the formulation of these rules, especially that of Miss Clara Beetle, Head of the Foreign Language Section, and Miss Edna M. Brown, Head of the Serials Section. Mr. C. Sumner Spalding, senior music cataloger, and a committee of music experts representing the Music Division, the Subject Cataloging Division, the Copyright Cataloging Division, and the Descriptive Cataloging Division are primarily responsible for the chapter on music which has been developed from the "preliminary version" of a *Code for Cataloging Music* issued by the Music Library Association in 1941. The rules for the cataloging of maps and atlases are based on a draft prepared by the Maps Division. Last, but far from least, thanks are due the members of the Committee on Descriptive Cataloging of the A. L. A. Division of Cataloging and Classification for their most helpful criticisms and suggestions.

LUCILE M. MORSCH, *Chief,*
Descriptive Cataloging Division

THE LIBRARY OF CONGRESS
Washington 25, D. C.
April 1949.

1. Introduction

DEFINITION OF DESCRIPTIVE CATALOGING

Cataloging of any kind and for any purpose involves some description of the object cataloged. Descriptive cataloging has been defined as "that phase of the process of cataloging which concerns itself with the identification and description of books." [1] The term is commonly used to distinguish that part of library cataloging which concerns itself with the identification and description of any item (not limited to "books") in the library's collection, from that part which involves the analysis of its subject content. This distinction has been the basis of the organization of cataloging in the Library of Congress, where the two component parts of cataloging are performed in a Descriptive Cataloging Division and a Subject Cataloging Division, respectively.

Although the preliminary second edition of the cataloging rules issued by the American Library Association in 1941, [2] by naming its two parts "Entry and heading," and "Description of book," respectively, has caused some ambiguity in the use of the term, "descriptive cataloging" is commonly understood to apply not only to the description of an item but also to the choice and determination of the form of the headings. That this latter phase of descriptive cataloging is not covered by the following principles and rules is to be attributed to the fact that the Library of Congress follows the A. L. A. rules for entry and heading; the scope of the following rules is, therefore, limited in general to that of part II of the A. L. A. rules of 1941.

HISTORY OF LIBRARY OF CONGRESS RULES

The rules which have been followed by the Library of Congress in its descriptive cataloging are easily traced to Charles A. Cutter's *Rules for a Dictionary Catalogue*, first published in 1876 as part II of the U. S. Bureau of Education's special report on *Public Libraries in the United States of America*. Rules in force at the Library of Congress prior to that date were followed until the end of 1899 when the card catalog which had been begun in 1865 was discontinued. This catalog consisted of 4½" x 7" cards bearing manuscript entries and mounted clippings from the earlier catalogs that were printed in book form. In July 1898 entries for books received by copyright were first printed and a new catalog on standard size cards (7½ x 12½ cm.) was started. For this work the rules adopted were those of Cutter with a few emendations from the A. L. A. catalog rules of 1883. At first the catalogers

---

[1] *A. L. A. Glossary of Library Terms.* Chicago, American Library Association, 1943.
[2] *A. L. A. Catalog Rules: Author and Title Entries.* Chicago, American Library Association, 1941.

3. Separately Published Monographs

3:1. PURPOSE

The purpose of cataloging a separately published monograph is to identify it and to distinguish it from other works and also from other editions of the same work and, in some instances, from other issues of the same edition. The description may also require that the nature and scope and the bibliographical history and relationships of the work be explained.

A. *Identification.* To distinguish one work from another, the title (together with the author's name as heading) is generally sufficient; for anonymous and pseudonymous works, other details, such as the statement which veils rather than names the author, or the imprint, are necessary in order to distinguish two works with the same title. To distinguish one edition from another of the same work, one or more of the following must be known: number or name of the edition, name of the editor, illustrator, translator, or publisher, date of publication, name of the series to which the edition belongs, or some detail of physical description such as the number of pages or volumes in the work. Since the user of the catalog rarely knows all of these details about the work he is seeking, and since in a growing library it cannot be foreseen which of them will be necessary to distinguish the various editions to be acquired, it is essential to include in each catalog entry all pertinent information of this type. (See 3:5–3:14, 3:16.)

To distinguish the various issues of a given edition, any of a wide variety of details may need to be specified. However, at the Library of Congress it is not the policy, except in certain cases of rare books, to collect the various issues of a given edition and consequently no attempt is made to describe works in detail sufficient to identify them as issues. Various issues are added to the collection as copies if the description of the first one cataloged fits those received later in all details or in all details except the imprint date [1] or the form of the publisher's name, or both. If there are other differences, the issues are generally treated as different editions. (See also Chapter 4, Issues, offprints, etc.)

B. *Description.* The elements in the catalog entry that identify the work and distinguish it from other works and other editions of the same work frequently supply all of the descriptive data that is necessary. Additional data may be necessary, however, to amplify or explain a title which is inadequate or misleading as to the nature or scope of the work, or to explain the bibliographical history and relationships of the work. (See 3:15 A.)

---

[1] A work that has a different copyright date is assumed to be a different edition even though all other elements of the description are the same.

3:2. ORGANIZATION OF THE DESCRIPTION

The basic part of the description, commonly called the "body of the entry," is presented in the first paragraph after the heading. It consists of the following elements for which this order of listing is *in general* prescribed: title, subtitle, author statement, edition statement (including statement of translator, illustrator or illustrations), and imprint. The second paragraph consists of the collation and series note. Any supplementary notes that may be necessary are presented in as many succeeding paragraphs as required.

3:3. SOURCE OF THE DESCRIPTION

In general, the items in the body of the entry and the series note represent the information presented by the work itself. The collation is the cataloger's description of the physical work and is limited to standard bibliographical terminology. The rest of the description may consist of statements quoted from the work or from other bibliographic sources, of statements phrased by the cataloger, or of a combination of the two if this results in the clearest and most concise statement.

3:4. RELATIONSHIP OF THE TITLE PAGE TO THE DESCRIPTION OF A WORK

The data given in the body of the entry are mainly those on the title page of the work, although certain items may be omitted and others may be added. Omissions made from the title, alternative title, or subtitle (except an initial article, see 3:5 A) are shown by the standard mark of omission, three dots; other omissions are not indicated. All additions of data, except punctuation and accents, are indicated by square brackets. If an addition is conjectural, it is so indicated by a question mark.

> [1946?]
> [Dublin? N. H.]
> Dublin [N. H.?]

Additions to the body of the entry are given in the language of the title page, except that the abbreviations "pseud.," "etc.," and "i. e." (and "et al." for foreign works in the Latin alphabet) are used.

If a statement that is included in the body of the entry is inaccurate, it is recorded as it appears, followed either by the word "sic" or by the abbreviation "i. e." and the correction.

If the sequence of statements on the title page varies significantly from the prescribed sequence (see 3:2) the prescribed order is observed by transposing to their proper positions the statements in question. Essential statements appearing elsewhere than on the title page may be inserted in their proper sequence.

The order of the title page is preferred if the variations from the prescribed sequence do not affect the title, subtitle or imprint. These are the only elements that have a fixed position in the catalog entry.

If the work does not have a title page to serve as the basis of the description, it is necessary to specify that a substitute has been used, unless the information has obviously been supplied by the cataloger. (See 3:4 A.) If there are several title pages one must be selected for use. (See 3:4 B.)

A. *Works without title pages.* A work that is published without a title page, or without a title page applying to the whole work (as in the case of some editions of the Bible or of many bilingual dictionaries), is cataloged from some other part of the work if possible and that part specified as the source of the data. The part of the work supplying the most complete information is used as the substitute, whether this be cover title, half-title, caption title, colophon, running title, or other part. Omissions and additions are indicated and transpositions made in the same manner as when the title page itself serves as the basis of the description.

If no part of the work supplies data that can be used as the basis of the description, the necessary information is taken from any available source, whether this be a reference work (which is preferable) or the content of the work itself. This is necessary for works the title pages of which are lost, collections of pamphlets or other minor material assembled by the Library or by a previous owner and which are to be cataloged as a single item, special numbers of periodicals without special titles which are to be cataloged as independent items, etc. Reprints of the several portions of a doctoral dissertation which together are considered by the university to which they were submitted as representing the published thesis, are cataloged as a single item under the title of the original thesis. In all such cases the entire body of the entry is enclosed in a single pair of brackets.

B. *Works with several title pages.* A monographic work in several volumes is, as a rule, cataloged from the title page of the first volume. Variations on the title pages of subsequent volumes are shown by incorporating the data with those from the first volume or by adding supplementary notes.

> The first ┌─second┐ canto of the Lusiad.
> Vol. 2 has subtitle: Statistics of housing.

A one-volume work with more than one title page is cataloged from the one that is most appropriate judged by the following considerations:

1. The first title page is preferred unless there is reason for choosing another.

2. If two title pages face each other, the second, which occupies the customary position of the title page, is preferred, unless one of the criteria in 3–8 below applies.

3. The title page bearing a later imprint date is preferred.

4. A printed title page is preferred to an engraved one since the latter may be used for various editions or issues of the work.

5. If the title pages present the work in different aspects (for example, as an individual work and as one volume of the author's complete works) the one which corresponds with the aspect in which the work is to be treated is chosen.

6. If there are title pages in more than one language, and text in but one language, the title page which is in the language of the text is preferred.

7. If there are title pages and text in more than one language, a title page that is in the original language of the work is preferred, unless a translation is known to be the reason for the publication, the original text being merely accessory to the translation.

8. Other things being equal, a title page is selected on the basis of language in the following order of preference: English, French, German, Spanish, Latin, any other language using the Latin alphabet, Greek, Russian, any other language using the Cyrillic alphabet, Hebrew, any other language using the Hebrew alphabet, any other language.

3:5. THE RECORDING OF THE TITLE

The title proper is transcribed exactly as to order, wording and spelling, but not necessarily as to punctuation and capitalization. Capitalization (see Appendix III) and punctuation in the catalog entry should follow as far as practicable the current usage of the language concerned. Accents are added in conformity with general usage (in French titles for books published after 1800, in Spanish, titles after 1890). Accents, but not umlauts, are to be omitted from capital letters and initials (except the French capital E). Unusual diacritical marks may be reproduced by specially made type or by additions in manuscript or they may be disregarded. Typographic peculiarities are disregarded; e. g., the use of v for u and i for j in works of the nineteenth and twentieth centuries. An "e" above a vowel in German words is replaced by an umlaut. Symbols and other matter that cannot be reproduced by the typographic facilities at the disposal of the Library are replaced by the cataloger's description.

> Funkenbusch, William.
>> The factorial function ₍Illustration of the symbol chosen to stand for factorial base₎ (n, d). ₍Houghton, Mich.₎ °1944.

Line endings are indicated only if all other methods of distinguishing two editions or issues of a rare book are inadequate, or to indicate that the title of such a book is printed in verse.

A. *Abridgment.* Long titles are abridged if this can be done without loss of essential information. The first words of the title are always included in the transcription except that an initial article is omitted if this will make it possible to omit the author statement that would otherwise be necessary (see 3:6) only because of the grammatical structure of the statement. For example, *The works of Shakespeare*, becomes

> Shakespeare, William, 1564–1616.
>> Works.

The article is not omitted if it is an essential part of the title. The first word of the title may be the name of the author. In the possessive form it is generally considered the author statement and omitted; it is retained if it appears as an integral part of the title; e. g., if it is the antecedent of a pronoun. Parts of the title more intelligibly presented in a contents paragraph are omitted from the transcription of the title. All omissions from the title, except the initial article, are indicated by a mark of omission.

B. *Titles in two or more languages.* If the title page has titles in two or more languages, the first title is recorded; if one of the succeeding titles is in English, it also is transcribed. The inclusion or omission of other titles depends upon the similarity of the titles in the various languages, the importance of the work cataloged, the presence of the original title of the work as a title other than the first, the language or languages of the text, and similar factors. The omission of one or more additional titles is not shown.

C. *Additions.* Additions may be made to the title in the language of the title if it needs explanation and if brief statements to clarify it can be taken from the work itself.

Titles in foreign languages using the Latin alphabet and which begin with a numeral (or which contain a numeral affecting the filing) have the word represented by the numeral, supplied.

> 30 ₍i. e. Třicet₎ hodin němčiny.
> 100 ₍i. e. Honderd₎ jaar spoorwegen in Nederland.
> 1842 ₍i. e. Mil ocho cientos cuarenta y dos₎: panorama y significación del movimiento literario.

Titles in other alphabets do not need the amplification because the word is substituted for the numeral in the "Title transliterated" note. (See 3:23.)

D. *Supplied titles.* If a title must be composed by the cataloger the nature and scope of the contents of the work are described as briefly as intelligibility permits.

E. *Alternative title.* An alternative title is always transcribed in the catalog entry because the book may be referred to by it and because another edition may be published with the alternative title as the title.

F. *Subtitle.* The subtitle is considered a part of the title and transcribed in the entry in the same manner as the title proper, except that a long subtitle which is separable from the title may be omitted and quoted in a supplementary note, if this increases the clarity of the entry. A subtitle preceding the title on the title page is transposed to the position determined by the general pattern of the catalog entry. Care must be exercised not to interpret a series statement or other data at the head of the title as a subtitle.

3:6. AUTHOR STATEMENT

The statement of authorship appearing on a work is incorporated in the catalog entry only if it is necessary for one of the following purposes:

a. To show variation in the form of name in the work from that adopted as the author heading, if the two are not obviously two forms of the same name.

> *Heading:* Liu, Ta-chün, 1890–
> *Author statement:* By D. K. Lieu.

b. To bring out the pseudonym under which an author has written.

c. To indicate the statement which veils rather than names the author of an anonymous work.

> By a lady.
> By a minister of the gospel.

d. To name the persons who contributed to a work of joint or composite authorship, and to show their part in the work.   (See 3:6 C.)

e. To show the relationship to the work of the person named in the heading (if this is other than author, editor, compiler, etc.) that otherwise would not be shown.

> **Nisenson, Samuel.**
> Giant book of sports, designed and illustrated by Samuel Nisenson.

f. To name the person or persons who prepared a work which is entered under a corporate author heading.

g. To name the corporate body with which the author is connected if this relationship needs to be stated to explain an added entry.

h. To make the title intelligible if the author's name is an integral part of the title.

A. *Transposition.* If the author statement is to be included in the entry and does not follow the title on the title page, it is transposed from the head of the title or elsewhere in the book to this position, with two exceptions: (a) if case endings would be affected by the transposition (see 3:17) and (b) if the statement of authorship, generally from within the book, involves an explanation which, because of its length or construction, is more satisfactorily presented in a supplementary note.

B. *Imprint as author statement.* If the fact of authorship is shown only by the name of the author (personal or corporate) in the imprint, and if the author statement is needed, the imprint is considered an adequate substitute for an author statement.

> **U. S.** *Bureau of Naval Personnel.*
> Naval justice. October 1945. ₁Washington₁ Standards and Curriculum Division, Training, Bureau of Naval Personnel ₁1945₁

14

C. *Joint authors.* Two or three joint authors, collaborators, or contributors are named in the author statement. If there are more than three, all after the first named are omitted. The omission is indicated as follows:

1. By the phrase "and others" if the title page is in English.

2. By the phrase "et al." if the title page is in any other language using the Latin alphabet.

3. By the equivalent of this phrase in the language of the title if the title page is not in the Latin alphabet; e. g., "и др." in Russian, "ואחרים" in Hebrew, and "און אנדערע" in Yiddish.

D. *Omissions from the author statement.*[2] Titles and abbreviations of titles of address, honor and distinction (but not of nobility), initials of societies, etc., are generally omitted from the author statement. Exception is made as follows:

1. If the title is necessary grammatically.

> Poesias del Sr. Dr. don Manuel Carpio con su biografía.

2. If the title is necessary for the identification of the author.

> By Mrs. Charles H. Gibson.

3. If the title explains the relationship of a personal author to the corporate author used as the heading for the work.

> By Luther H. Evans, Librarian of Congress.

E. *Additions to the author statement.* If necessary for intelligibility, a word or phrase in the language of the title is added to express what is shown on the title page by arrangement, or to clarify an ambiguous or misleading statement.

> L'aviation ⟨par⟩ Paul Painlevé ⟨et⟩ Émile Borel.

If a pseudonymous work is entered under the real name of the author, the designation "pseud." is added after the pseudonym in the author statement, unless the pseudonym is in the possessive case. (See 3:24.)

3:7. EDITION

The edition of a work is always described in its catalog entry, the impression or printing only in the case of items having particular bibliographical importance. This makes it necessary for the cataloger to be aware of the lack of uniformity among publishers in the use of the terms "edition" and "impression" or "printing" and their equivalents in other languages, and to interpret them according to the accepted definitions. In case of doubt as to whether the terms "edition," "edizione," etc., refer to an edition or an issue of a work, the statement is given in its customary position, following the title or author statement.

If the volumes in a set are of different editions, the edition statement is generally

---

[2] Similar omissions are made from statements of editors, illustrators, translators, etc., whether these are included in the body of the entry, in contents, or in other notes.

omitted from the body of the entry and the various editions are specified in a supplementary note or in the list of contents.

> On,cover, v. 1: 3. éd.; v. 2: 2. éd.
> CONTENTS.—1. deel. Klankleer, woordvorming, aard en verbuiging der woorden. 4. uitg. 1871.—2. deel. Leer van den volzin (syntaxis) 2. uitg. 1863.—3. deel. Stijlleer. (Rhetorica, letterkundige encyclopaedie en kritiek) 2. verm. uitg. 1880.

3:8. STATEMENT OF THE NUMBER OF VOLUMES

A statement of the number of volumes in a work is specified in its catalog entry, between the title and the imprint, only if such a statement appearing on the work is at variance with the information shown in the collation of the work. The discrepancy is necessarily explained.

3:9. ILLUSTRATION STATEMENT

The statement of the illustrative matter appearing on the title page of a work is included in the catalog entry only if it adds an important characterization of the material that cannot be shown in the collation; e. g., the number of illustrations in a work containing many unnumbered plates or text illustrations, the kind of illustrations (such as photographs or engravings), or the name of the artist.

3:10. IMPRINT

The place of publication, name of the publisher and date of publication, which constitute the imprint of a work, serve both to identify and to characterize the work. Different editions are most commonly distinguished by the differences in their imprints. The place of publication, particularly if it is not a large publishing center, may suggest a probable local viewpoint of the author. The publisher's name may also suggest a viewpoint or bias (especially when the publisher is a society or institution) or may be an indication of the quality either of the subject matter or the physical make-up of the work. The date generally indicates the timeliness of the subject matter.

The imprint is recorded in the catalog entry in the conventional order of place, publisher, date.

A. *Works with more than one place and publisher.* A work that gives indication of being published in several places by one publisher or by several publishers, is described in the catalog entry by an imprint consisting of the first named place of publication and the corresponding publisher, unless there is reason to use another or to use more than one.

If a place or publisher that is not the first named is distinguishable by type or position, or otherwise, as the actual or principal place or publisher, it is given in the catalog entry; in this case the first-named place or publisher is omitted.

If a city in the United States, with or without an American publisher, is named in a secondary position on a title page containing a foreign imprint, it is included in addition to the foreign imprint.

> London, New York, Longmans, Green.
> Paris, Gauthier-Villars; Chicago, University of Chicago Press.

B. *Printer's imprint as a substitute for publisher's imprint.* A work with place of publication and publisher unknown has the place of printing and the name of the printer used in the imprint in the catalog entry if they are on the title page [1] or are of special bibliographical importance. (See 3: 10 C.) The place of publication is not combined with the name of the printer, nor the place of printing with the name of the publisher. It is well to be conscious of the fact that some printing establishments are also publishers; e. g., the U. S. Govt. Print. Off.

C. *Supplied imprint.* If the imprint data are not found in the work itself but can be ascertained by a reasonable search in other sources, they are supplied; the language of the title page is employed if this form is available. However, no effort is made to ascertain the imprint data for offprints or separates. If the place of publication is not known, the place of printing is used as the probable place of publication; if neither is known, the place is represented by the abbreviation "n. p." for "no place." Lack of a publisher is not indicated. If the date is not known and cannot be approximated, it is represented by "n. d." for "no date." The abbreviations are enclosed in brackets.

D. *Inflections in imprint.* Place names or names of publishers appearing in the imprint in an inflected form or with an accompanying preposition which affects the case ending of the name are so recorded in the catalog entry. (See also 3: 12.)

> Berolini
> V Praze
> Im Deutschen Verlag

E. *Fictitious and imaginary imprints.* A fictitious or imaginary imprint may be recorded in the catalog entry either in the conventional order or in the form in which it appears on the title page of the work, depending upon which one results in the more intelligible statement. It is followed by the actual imprint if this can be supplied.

> Paris, Impr. Vincent, 1798 [i. e. Bruxelles, Moens, 1883]
> Imprimé a cent lieves de la Bastille. [Londres] 1771.

F. *Hebrew and Yiddish works.* A Hebrew or Yiddish imprint, or the part of it that is in Hebrew characters, is followed by an imprint in one of the other languages for which the Library has printing facilities if it can be found in the work being cataloged. If there is no such imprint in the work, the place of publication is supplied using the English equivalent of the name. If an equivalent name in English is not known, the name is supplied in the vernacular of the place.

---

[1] The name of the printer is omitted from the imprint of a thesis even if given on the title page.

3:11. PLACE OF PUBLICATION

The place of publication is the place in which the offices of the publisher are located. It is commonly designated on the title pages of his publications, immediately preceding or following his name.

If the place of publication is unknown, the location of the editorial office, or the seat of the institution, or headquarters of the society publishing the work, is to be given in the imprint of the catalog entry in preference to the place of printing. The place of residence of the editor should not be confused with the location of an editorial office.

A. *Additions to place name.* The place of publication is followed by its country, state or similar designation if it is necessary to identify the place or to distinguish it from another place of the same name. Abbreviations are used for most such designations (see Appendix III). Similarly, if the place of publication is a section or a suburb of a city, the name of the city may have to be added.

B. *Abbreviated place names.* The name of a city which is abbreviated in the imprint on the title page is abbreviated in the catalog entry. If required for clarity, the abbreviated form is completed or followed by the full form.

> Rio ¡de Janeiro¡
> Mpls ¡i. e. Minneapolis¡

C. *Places with changed names.* If the name of the place of publication is changed, or if the place is incorporated into a larger unit, during the publication of a work in several volumes, the form of the name appearing on the first volume, followed (in parentheses) by the later name or names appearing on succeeding volumes, is used for the imprint in the catalog entry.

> Christiania (Oslo)

3:12. PUBLISHER

The publisher statement appearing on a work is abridged as much as possible without loss of intelligibility or identification of the publisher. Unnecessary parts of the statement are omitted, abbreviations are employed (see Appendix III), and names known to be forenames are represented by initials[4] or, in the case of well-known publishers, omitted. If the personal name of the publisher is sufficient for intelligibility, and for identification of the publisher, it is given in the nominative case whether it appears in that form or in the possessive.

A. *Unnecessary parts of the publisher statement.* The following parts are generally considered unnecessary: (1) the phrases "published by," "published for," and the word "publisher," and their equivalents in other languages, (2) words showing that the publisher is also the printer or bookseller, (3) the initial article,

---

[4] Forenames of persons in whose honor a firm is named are spelled in full; for example, Stephen Daye Press, *not* S. Daye Press.

18

except when necessary for clarity, (4) the phrases "and company," "and sons," etc., and their foreign equivalents, (5) terms meaning "incorporated" or "limited" and their abbreviations, (6) either the name of the press or the name of the publisher if both are used, the second named generally being omitted, (7) either the initialism (or abbreviation) of a corporate name or the name it represents if they are used together, the full form being omitted if it appears in any other place in the catalog entry, (8) the name of the director or founder of a publishing concern, and (9) the name of the publishing firm if it is used with the name of a branch or division identified with the publication of a particular type of book; e. g., McGraw-Hill and its branch, Whittlesey House.

B. *Essential parts of the publisher statement.* Data that are considered necessary for the intelligibility of the publisher statement include the following:

1. Words or phrases indicating that the name in the imprint is not that of the publisher.

> Impr. de C. Gómez.
> In Kommission bei O. Harrassowitz.
> Printed by the G. Banta Pub. Co.
> Planographed by Edwards Bros.

2. Both the publisher and his agent when both are named.

> London, The Society; sold by Longman.

3. Phrases indicating the official status of a government printer, or the official authorization of a commercial printer.

4. The names of both firms if one has responsibility for editorial supervision and the other for manufacture and distribution.

5. The names of both publisher and printer for works from the sixteenth through the eighteenth and early nineteenth centuries, before the functions of printer, publisher and bookseller had assumed their modern differentiation, if both are named on the work.

6. The statement that a work is privately printed.

7. Phrases showing that the publisher is also the author of the work, if a author statement is needed. (See 3:6 and 3:12 C.)

8. The name of the publishing body in both transliterated (or vernacular) and translated form when both are used on the work. When the name appears in several languages, the recording of it in the catalog entry is governed by the rule for recording a title in more than two languages. (See 3:5 B.)

C. *Omission of publisher.* For a work entered under a corporate author heading with the same body responsible both for authorship and for publication, the publisher statement is omitted from the imprint. If the responsibility for authorship is shown only by the publisher statement and the name in this statement varies essentially from the form of the name adopted for the heading, the publisher statement is omitted from the imprint and the information given in a supplementary note.

> Published by the society under its earlier name:

3:13. DATE

The imprint date on the title page is generally given as the date of publication. If the year in which the work was actually put on sale or distributed to the public is known to differ from the date on the title page, it is added after the other in the catalog entry.

1947 ¡i. e. 1946¡

A. *Multiple volume works.* If the work is in more than one volume and the publication dates of the individual volumes vary, the inclusive dates are given in the imprint. This rule is to apply also if the volumes are irregularly dated. Inclusive dates in the same century are given in the form 1923–30. The latest publication date is not bracketed if it appears on the title page of the volume then published. If the date of the first or the last volume does not correspond with the respective year given in the imprint, the irregularity is shown in the form 1923–30 ¡v. 1, 1930¡

B. *Loose-leaf volumes and works published in parts.* If the work is a loose-leaf volume designed to receive additions, or is a work issued in parts, and is cataloged while the work is in progress of being published, the date is left open; e. g., 1944–   . When the entry is closed the inclusive dates of publication are shown. A later title page replacing the original one may require that the date be changed, the form becoming 1946 ¡i. e. 1944¡–47, or 1947 ¡i. e. 1944–47¡

C. *Dates not of the Christian era.* If the only imprint date on the title page is not a year of the Christian era it is given as it appears followed by the date of the Christian era.

Roma, anno xviii ¡1939¡

If the chronology does not coincide with the Christian year, and the month and day of publication are not known, the form 1881/82 is used.

D. *Chronograms.* If the date of publication occurs as a chronogram in the title or in the imprint it is transcribed as it appears. If the chronogram is lengthy or involved it is omitted. In either case the date is supplied in arabic numerals in the imprint. For example, if the imprint date is revealed in a chronogram reading "To aLL MaRshaLLs aLL oVer the VVorLD I beqVeath thIs VVork gratIs," the date 1883 is supplied. This date was obtained by considering the large capitals to be roman numerals and by adding them together.

E. *Date uncertain.* If there is no date of publication given in the book and the exact date cannot be ascertained, an approximate date is supplied as follows:

¡1892 or 3¡ one of two years certain.
¡1892?¡ probable date.
¡ca. 1892¡ approximate date.
¡189–¡ decade certain.
¡189–?¡ decade uncertain.
¡18—¡ century certain.
¡n. d.¡ century uncertain.

F. *Copyright data.* If the date or probable date of publication of a copyrighted work is not ascertained, the date given in the copyright notice, preceded by a "c," is given. If the date in this statement is not the same as the date on the title page or the actual date of publication, as supplied, both dates are given.

    ₁1946₁ •1945.
    ₁1946, •1945₁
    1946 ₁•1945₁
    1947, •1946–48.
    1947–48, •1946–47.

G. *Other qualified dates.* If the date, or probable date of publication within a decade, is not ascertained, and the work does not bear a copyright date, the date may be taken from the preface, introduction, dedication, etc., or from the cover. In each such case, however, the date must be qualified in the imprint.

    ₁pref. 1889₁
    ₁cover 1935₁
    ₁Vorwort 1908₁

If the date on the cover varies from that given on the title page, both dates are recorded in the imprint (e. g., 1932 ₁cover 1934₁) unless the cover date is known to be the true date of publication. The date is then recorded as a correction.

3:14. COLLATION

The collation is the cataloger's description of the physical work and consists of a statement of the extent of the work in pages or volumes, the important illustrative matter, and the size. The terms used are those for which accepted definitions are available rather than those of the author or publisher, if there is any conflict between the two.

A. *Extent of text in one volume.* In describing the extent of a work that is complete in one volume, the terminology suggested by the work is followed as far as possible. That is, a work with leaves printed on both sides is described in terms of pages, one with the leaves printed on only one side, in terms of leaves. A work which has numbered pages and unnumbered leaves is described only in terms of pages, one that has numbered leaves and unnumbered pages is described only in terms of leaves. A work without numbering is described in terms of either pages or leaves, but not of both. Books printed before the eighteenth century with leaves printed on both sides but numbered as leaves are described in terms of leaves. A work printed with more than one column to a page, the columns instead of the pages being number' ' is described in terms of columns. A folder, a broadside, and a sheet are ˰˰ ˰ed in the collation.

In recording the number of pages, leaves, or columns, the indication in the work (whether roman or arabic numbers, or letters) is followed. In describing a work with pages lettered rather than numbered, the inclusive letters are specified; for example, a–x p. or A–K p. or a–d leaves. Pages or leaves numbered in words, or in characters other than arabic or roman, are designated in the collation in arabic figures.

The last numbered page or leaf of each paged section is recorded, the numbers being separated by commas. A section is either a separately numbered group of pages, or an unnumbered group which, because of its length (one fifth or more of the entire work), or its importance, should be mentioned. Separately paged and unpaged sections consisting of advertising matter are disregarded. (See 3:15.) If it is necessary to refer in a supplementary note to unnumbered pages that would not otherwise be covered by the colla'ion, this statement is elaborated to include the unnumbered group of pages.

> 365, ₍3₎ p.
> Bibliography: p. 363–₍367₎
>
> ₍8₎. 155 p.
> Bibliography: 6th prelim. page.

The last numbered page or leaf should represent the total number, or approximately the total number, of pages or leaves in the work or in the section. If it does not, a correction may be necessary. For example, (a) if only the alternate pages are numbered the collation may read 48 (i. e. 96) p., (b) if the final page is typographically incorrect the collation may read 329 (i. e. 392) p. If the numbering changes from roman to arabic numerals within the sequence this fact is ignored. For example, a work with pages numbered i–viii, 9–176 is described simply as 176 p. Inclusive paging is given for works that seem to be incomplete or which are merely parts of a larger work.

> 5?–140 p.
> ?1–378 p.

1. *Unpaged works.* Works printed without pagination or foliation are described as ₍v.₎ (unpaged) unless the total number of pages or leaves is easily ascertained.

2. *Complicated or irregular paging.* Any of three ways of describing works with complicated or irregular paging may be chosen, depending upon the extent of the complications: (a) to record, in brackets, the total number [*] of pages or leaves in the work; this is done for works of less than 100 pages and for other works if they are important and cannot be described according to either (b) or (c); (b) to record the number of pages or leaves in one or more main sections of the work and the total number, in brackets, of the remaining variously paged and unpaged sections (xiv, 226, ₍44₎ p.); (c) to describe the work simply as 1 v. (various pagings). All loose-leaf publications in one volume which are *designed to receive additions* are described as 1 v. (loose-leaf) even though the pagination at the time of cataloging is not complicated or irregular.

---

[*] The count begins with the first printed page and ends with the last printed page, exclusive of advertising matter; intermediate blank pages but not blank leaves are counted.

3. *Folded leaves.* Folded leaves of text are so described unless the work is bibliographically unimportant.

> 17 fold. l.
> [37] l. (3 fold.)

4. *Double leaves.* If numbered pages are printed on a double leaf, Chinese and Japanese style, they are described as pages or leaves according to their numbering as pages or leaves; if unnumbered, each double leaf is counted as two pages.

> 36 p. (on double leaves)
> 18 double l.
> [36] p. (on double leaves)

5. *Duplicate paging.* If the paging is duplicated, which is not unusual in books with text in two languages, both pagings are recorded and an explanation is added:

> xii, 35, 35 p.
> Opposite pages numbered in duplicate.

6. *Two numberings.* If a work has a pagination of its own and also bears the pagination of a larger work of which it is a part, the separate paging is recorded in the collation and the continuous paging in a supplementary note.

7. *Two-way paging.* If, in works with texts in two languages one of which reads from left to right, the other from right to left (e. g., Hebrew), the texts are in two distinct sections, and the page sequence is from opposite ends to the center of the book, both groups of paging are recorded as if for separate works. Paging of the part the title of which has been chosen for the catalog entry is given first. The two groups of paging are separated by a semicolon.

> ix, 115 p.; x, 127 p.

8. *Columns.* If an unpaged work is printed in numbered columns, two or more to a page, the number of columns is given in the collation.

> xx p., 1660 columns.

9. *Music in collation.* If, in a work which is not entirely music, an unpaged or separately paged section consists of music, these pages or leaves are designated as music in the collation, following the number of pages of text.

> 74 p., music (15 p.)

If the music occurs in scattered groups of pages or leaves not independently numbered, it is generally described in a supplementary note rather than in the collation.

10. *Incomplete copies.* If the last part of a work is wanting, and the paging of a complete copy cannot be ascertained, paging is given in the form 179+ p., with note of the imperfection.

> xxiv, 179+ p.
> L. C. copy imperfect: all after p. 179 wanting.

B. *Extent of text in more than one volume.* The number of bibliographical volumes or parts of a work in more than one volume is shown in the collation. If this number differs from the number of physical volumes, both are stated, the bibliographical volumes first.

> 8 v. in 5.

If the work is paged continuously, the pagination is indicated, in parentheses, following the number of volumes, according to the rule for indicating the pagination of a work that is complete in one volume. Separately paged preliminary matter in volumes after the first is ignored unless it is important; if it is important, the work is not considered as being paged continuously.

> 2 v. (xxxi, 999 p.)

In addition to volumes, the following terms are used in the collation to describe works in more than one volume or part:

> *Parts*—for bibliographical units of a work intended to be bound several to the volume, especially if so designated by the publisher.
>
> *Pamphlets*—for collections of pamphlets bound together or assembled in a portfolio for cataloging as a collection.
>
> *Pieces*—for items of varying character (pamphlets, broadsides, clippings, maps, etc.) published or assembled as a collection.

C. *Illustrative matter.* Brief mention of the illustrative matter in a work comprises the second part of the collation statement. The abbreviation "illus.," for illustrations, is used to describe all types of illustrative matter except maps * and portraits unless other particular types in the work are considered important enough to be specifically designated. If the illustrative matter is limited to an illustrated title page or to minor illustration it is generally disregarded.

The most common types of illustrative matter are designated in the following order: illustrations, plates (specified only if they are an important feature of the work), portraits (or group portraits, but not both), maps. Other terms less frequently used (charts, coats of arms, diagrams, facsimiles, forms, genealogical tables, music, photographs, plans, profiles, samples, tables, typographical specimens, etc.) follow in alphabetical order. (See Appendix III, Abbreviations.) A frontispiece is described as such if it is the only illustration in the work and if it cannot be better described by type of illustration.

1. *Colored illustrative matter.* Important illustrative matter that is printed with ink in two or more colors (counting black as a color), or part of which is so printed, is described as colored.

> col. illus., maps (part col.)

2. *Illustrative matter on folded leaves.* Folded maps are specified as "fold. maps" in collation; other plates are specified as folded only if the folding is an important feature (e. g., a panoramic view).

> fold. col. facsim.

---

* Maps in works of belles-lettres, in children's books, and in textbooks intended for elementary or secondary schools are described as illustrations.

3. *Mounted illustrative matter.* Important mounted illustrations, whether or not they are figures in the text, are described in collation as mounted illustrations. The term "mounted plates" is not used. Mounted samples are specified as such whether they are plates or within the text.

> mounted col. illus.

4. *Number of illustrations recorded.* The number of illustrations, plates, portraits, maps, etc., may be specified in the collation if it can be readily ascertained or verified from the work itself (i. e., when the illustrations or plates are listed, or their number is stated) but only if the book or illustration warrants such description. If the number is given for a work with several plate numberings, only the total number is recorded. Arabic numerals are used.

If plates of various types have a comprehensive numbering they may be specified as follows:

> 20 plates (ports., facsims., music)
> 20 plates (incl. ports.)
> 20 plates (incl. 4 ports.)

5. *Illustrative matter in pockets or portfolios.* Maps, or other illustrative matter, issued in a pocket inside the cover of a work, or issued separately in a portfolio, are mentioned in the collation and their location designated. The number of separate pieces is generally specified.

> 3 charts (in pocket)
> illus., maps (4 fold. col. in pocket)
> 100 col. maps (2 fold. in pocket)
> 36 p.   24 plates (in portfolio)

If, however, more than one type of illustration specified in the collation is represented by items in the pocket, a general note is used instead.

> Illustrative matter in pocket.
> Part of illustrative matter in pocket.

6. *Illustrations with little or no text.* A work consisting of illustrations with little or no continuous text is described in the same manner as other works except that the two parts of the collation devoted to paging and the illustrative matter are combined.

> 35 p., 120 p. of illus.
> 120 p. (chiefly illus., ports., maps)
> [2] l., 72 plates (in portfolio)
> 1 v. (chiefly illus., maps)

D. *Size.* The size of the work is included in the catalog entry as an aid in finding the work on the shelves and as an aid to the user of the catalog in selecting a desirable edition. It also serves the reader who wishes to borrow the work through interlibrary loan or who wishes to order a photocopy of the work or a part of it.

The height of the work is given in centimeters, exact to within one centimeter, fractions of a centimeter being counted as a full centimeter. For example, a work which measures 17.2 centimeters is described as 18 cm. Miniature books, those ten centimeters or less in height, are described in millimeters, exact to the nearest millimeter. In describing bound volumes, the height of the binding is measured.

The width of the work is also specified if it is less than half the height or if it is greater than the height. The height is given first, in the following form: 20 x 8 cm. or 20 x 32 cm.

Both height and width are specified in the collation of broadsides and other single sheets. If the sheet is designed for issue in folded format, as indicated by data on outside when folded, or by part of the material being imposed as pages, the dimensions of the sheet as folded are also given, in the following form: 48 x 30 cm. fold. to 24 x 15 cm. If the sheet is intended to be used only in the folded form, it is described as a folder, followed by the number of imposed pages, rather than as a sheet; only the folded size is given.

> folder (8 p.)   18 cm.

If there is a difference of less than two centimeters in the size of the volumes of a set, the larger size is given in the collation. If the difference is of two or more centimeters, the inclusive sizes are given; e. g., 24–27 cm. For a set with a single variation in size the prevailing size is given, followed by the variation, in the following form: 27 cm. (v. 1–3: 34 cm.).

In cataloging a volume consisting of pamphlets or other works of different size bound together, the size of the bound volume is given.

E. *Atlases accompanying text volumes.* Volumes or portfolios consisting of plates and not numbered consecutively with the other volumes of a set are specified separately in the collation. The statement precedes the size unless the size of the atlas volume or portfolio differs from that of the rest of the set, and must, therefore, also be given.

> 3 v.   and atlas (30 plates)   30 cm.
> 169 p.   and atlas (3 l., 18 plates)   28 cm.
> 3 l., 100 p.   illus.   25 cm.   and portfolio (24 plates)   30 cm.
> 6 v.   illus., maps.   and 3 atlases (plates, maps)   22 cm.
> 9 v. in 11.   plates, maps.   and atlas (2 v.   maps)   26 cm.

If, however, the title of the atlas or portfolio differs from that of the main work, if there is a special compiler, or if some other feature requires further description, the "dash" form of entry adopted for supplements is preferred. (See Chapter 5, Supplements, indexes, etc.).

3:15. NOTES

Data to be included in the catalog entry to amplify the formalized description presented according to the preceding rules may be combined with the formalized part of the entry or added in the form of supplementary notes. Such data are incorporated in the body of the entry only to the extent that the rules for the

preparation of this part of the entry provide. The limitation is necessary if the advantages of a formalized description are not to be lost.

Inclusion of special data in the collation statement is limited to matters of physical description closely related to the items of the collation (i. e., pages or volumes, illustrative matter, and size) and which can be stated briefly. Certain types of such notes have been suggested in the rules for collation; others are suggested by the following examples.

> 124 p. (p. 119–124 advertisements)
>> (*The advantage of including all of this information in the collation is that, since the section of advertising follows the text, the work may also be described as having 118 pages, or it may even be issued also without the advertising. The explanation in juxta-position with the full paging shows immediately that another edition is not involved.*)

> 34 p. (incl. cover)
>> (*A copy that has lost its cover, possibly in binding, may appear to be complete in 32 pages, and, as in the case above, be considered a different edition.*)

Other notes may be either conventional in style, following, as far as possible, set forms and generally fixed positions in the catalog entry, or miscellaneous or informal notes, consisting of statements quoted from the work or other sources, or expressed by the cataloger in his own words, or of a combination of the two.

A. *Kinds of notes.* Conventional notes are used in order (1) to name the series of which the work is a part (3:16), (2) to specify certain information that appears at the head of the title (3:17), (3) to indicate other works bound with the one described (3:18), (4) to name sequels to the work (3:19), (5) to show that the work is an academic dissertation or other academic publication (3:20–3:21), (6) to specify the contents of the work or a part of it (3:22), (7) to indicate the transliteration of a title not in the Latin alphabet (3:23), (8) to indicate the full name of the author if a shortened form of the name is used for the heading, or the real name if an assumed name is adopted for the heading (3:24).

Informal notes are used for any other data that need to be specified. In general they fall into two categories: notes that contribute to the identification of the work, thereby being given a prominent position in the catalog entry (see C 1–6 below), and notes that describe or characterize the work and tell its bibliographical history (see C 7–9 below).

Although rules are necessary for the preparation of notes in conventional style, they cannot be written to cover informal notes. The following general principles, however, can be stated to guide the cataloger in formulating them.

Supplementary notes are added to the catalog entry only if the data they supply cannot be satisfactorily integrated with the data in the body of the entry or in the collation.

Notes are as brief as clarity and good grammatical usage will permit.

Notes are factual and unbiased and do not state critical judgments of the cataloger.

Notes consist of references to bibliographical sources if satisfactory descriptions can be cited, to avoid making lengthy notes.

The value of each note is considered in relation to the resulting length of the whole catalog entry.

The authority for the spelling of the words that are not quoted is Webster's *New International Dictionary of the English Language.*

The sources of the data supplied in notes are cited in accordance with the general principles of descriptive cataloging. The form of the citation is as follows:

The source of a quoted note is preceded by a dash, the source of a statement not quoted by "Cf." The source, not included within quotation marks, consists of the author's name, in direct form, and the title in sufficient fullness for identification without a key. Commonly used and easily recognizable words are abbreviated. (See Appendix III.) If page references are given, the source of the citation is specified by edition, or by place and date of publication.

B. *Order of notes.* Various considerations affect the order of notes, making an arbitrary order undesirable. However, notes covered by 1–4 above are given first and in that order. In certain cases, various notes are grouped together to produce a clear, logical entry; for example, in cataloging a facsimile reproduction of an early work, the notes referring to the original edition are grouped and separated from the notes referring specifically to the reproduction.

C. *Examples of informal notes.*

1. Source of title.

> Caption title.[7]
> Title from first line of text.

2. Imperfections in the copy.

> L. C. copy imperfect: t. p. wanting; title from cover.
> L. C. copy imperfect: p. 7–16 wanting; photocopy supplied from a copy in the John Carter Brown Library.
> L. C. set incomplete: v. 12 wanting.

3. Title page information not incorporated in the body of the entry.

> Slip mounted on t. p. changes the title to: A correct history of Grant at the Battle of Shiloh.
> Imprint on mounted label.
> Imprint covered by label: Zürich, Humanitas-Verlag.
> Original imprint covered by label, as above.
> Series no. corrected in ms.
> Vol. 1: 4th ed., 1905; v. 2: 2d ed., 1906; v. 3: 1905.

4. Variations from the title page title appearing elsewhere in the work; **a variant cover title, caption title, or running title by which the work might be known or identified**, or which explains the title chosen, variations in the title in a work in several volumes, and added title pages giving information varying from or supplementing the title page.

> Cover title: The fair American.
> _____ (*Title page title: The adventures of Emmera, or, The fair American.*)

[7] Not used in cataloging broadsides or other material limited to one leaf.

Vol. 2 has title:
Added t. p., engr., with imprint date 1822.
Added t. p., in French.
Vol. 1 has added t. p., with imprint:

5. Physical description, supplementing the collation, to show that the actual amount of text is not correctly suggested by the collation, that there is text on covers, guard sheets, plates, etc., to show peculiarities and irregularities, to describe format, limited editions (i. e., editions consisting of 500 copies or less) large paper copies, etc.

Alternate pages blank.

Printed on one side of leaf.

(*Used for a work published before 1700, when leaves were normally printed on both sides.*)

Pages 65–98, advertising matter [or coordinate paper, blank for "Notes," etc.]

(*Such a section is ignored unless it occupies more than one fifth of the total number of pages or appears at the end of the work.*)

Text on versos of plates.

(*Such a note is used only if the paging suggests very little text and there is a relatively large amount on the plates.*)

Pages also numbered 35–89, continuing the paging of the preceding number.

Pages 193–203 numbered 223–233.

Map on lining-paper.

(*Used if such a map is the only one in the work; on which lining-paper is not specified.*)

Plates engraved by _____ after drawings by _____.

Signatures:

(*Used only for unpaged works bearing signature numbering, or for paged works to distinguish two issues or editions with the same final pagination.*)

Printed on vellum.

"300 copies printed in Perpetus type on Arnold's hand-made paper. No. 8."

"555 exemplaires numérotés ... 5 exemplaires sur papier du Japon: 1 à 5, avec un quadruple état du frontispice." No. 5.

640 copies printed. "Trente exemplaires sur pur fil Lafuma numérotés de I à xxx, plus dix exemplaires hors commerce, numérotés de 31 à 40 (H. C.)" No. xxx.

"Large paper copy."

Facsimile reproduction of ms. copy.

Photocopy of composer's ms.

6. Statement of limited distribution or non-commercial nature of the publication.

"For official use only."

7. Nature and scope of work and literary form, if the title is misleading and not clarified by the secondary entries traced; language of text, if the language of the title differs from that of the text, or if for any other reason the language of

the text is not obvious. Literary form is not indicated for a classic nor ordinarily for fiction.

> Textbook for grade three.
> An advertisement for the Bell Telephone Co.
> To 1914. Later memoirs, "in preparation," were not published.
> Prose translation.
> Fictionized biography.
> German and English; added t. p. in English.
> Translated from the author's unpublished ms.

8. Notes on authorship, editors, etc., to document the heading or added entries or to supplement the title page information.

> Authors' names in reverse order in other editions.
>
> Has been erroneously ascribed to Mrs. Slack (i. e. Ann Fisher Slack) who wrote under the name A. Fisher. Cf. Brit. Mus. Cat.; Halkett and Laing; L. C. Karpinski. The elusive George Fisher. 1935.
>
> Also attributed to Jonathan Swift. Cf. Evans. Amer. bibl.
>
> "Also attributed to Jonathan Swift."—Evans. Amer. bibl.
>
> Based on Sir William MacNaghten's edition of the Arabic text (Calcutta, Thacker, 1839–42)

9. Bibliographical history; relationship to other works (predecessors, successors, sequels, revisions which are substantially new works, supplements, indexes, commentaries, criticisms, concordances, abridgments, adaptations, dramatizations, parodies, etc.) and to other editions of the same work. These include:

The original or earliest known title of a work reissued in the same language with a changed title, except for the works of classical authors for which a special filing scheme has been adopted. The statement is worded to include all earlier editions if this can be done with brevity and without further search.

> First ed. published in 1934 under title:
> Previous editions published under title:

The titles of one or more other editions in the same language, if it cannot be ascertained which is the earlier.

> American ed. (New York, Knopf) has title:
> London ed. (Collins) has title:

The original title of a translated work if the title of the translation is not a literal translation of the original title; if the original title is in a language that does not employ the Latin alphabet, a transliteration of it is added.

> Translation of
> Translation of Ha дне (transliterated: Na dne)

Information that a work in a foreign language has been issued also in English, if neither is known to be a translation of the other.

> Issued also in English.

The title of the edition in the language of the heading or the native tongue of the

author, if a work is issued in several languages at the same time and without indication of the original, unless the titles are literal translations.

> Issued also under title:

The author or editor of earlier or subsequent editions if there has been a change of author heading within a series of consecutively numbered editions.

Information in regard to the original publication of works which first appeared as part of another publication, if this can be given in a specific form leading to the earlier work.

> From the author's Unterhaltungen deutscher Ausgewanderten.
>
> "Reprinted from the Physical review, vol. 70, nos. 5–6 ... September 1–15, 1946."

The location of the original work from which a photo copy has been reproduced. (See Chapter 10, Facsimiles, photocopies and microfilms.)

The manuscript source of a work if the manuscript's designation in a manuscript collection may be used in citing the work.

> The first play in the so-called "Parnassus trilogy," reproduced in facsimile from a unique ms. in the Bodleian (Rawlinson. D. 398)
>
> The original, Ms. IV.A.3 in the Biblioteca nazionale, Naples, contains the second and only remaining portion of the abridgment by Festus of the lost treatise, De verborum significatu, of M. Verrius Flaccus.

3:16. SERIES NOTES

The series note gives the information that a work is part of a series of publications issued under a collective title. It is given in the catalog entry immediately following the collation, enclosed within parentheses. If the statement does not appear anywhere in the work being cataloged, and is supplied from some other source, it is enclosed in brackets.

The series statement on the work may include, in addition to the title of the series (in one or more languages), the name of an editor or editors, and the number of the volume, if the series consists of consecutively numbered volumes or parts. If all of the parts of the series are by the same author, personal or corporate, this fact is generally shown.

The series note includes all of this information except the names of editors. The form of the note follows the statement on the work, except that the number of the series is placed at the end of the note unless this would involve a transposition affecting grammatical structure. If the series title appears in more than one language, one of which agrees with the title of the monograph, this title is chosen for the series note.

> (Typophile chap books, 7)
>
> (Britain advances ₁10₁)
>
> (McEvoy's essentials of geography, no. 4)
>
> (Geological Society of America. Special paper no. 6)

(Suomalais-ugrilaisen Seuran Noimituksea, 59. Mémoires de la Société finno-ougrienne, 59)

(Ergänzungsheft zum Deutschen statistischen Zentralblatt, 7)

A. *Works in several volumes.* If the work being cataloged is in several volumes in a numbered series, the series volume numbers are given in an inclusive form (e. g., v. 11-15) or to indicate the broken sequence (e. g., v. 131, 145, 152)

B. *Series title in two forms.* If the series title appears on the work in more than one form, the form that is used for the entry of the series in the catalog is selected for the series note. The varying form is noted if it appears to be of value for identification.

C. *Series title combined with the monograph title.* A series statement occurring in combination with the monograph title is separated, if possible, from the title and given in the regular series position.

From morality to religion, being the Gifford lectures delivered at the University of St. Andrews, 1938.

Title: From morality to religion.

Series: (Gifford lectures, 1938)

D. *Series of works by one author.* If all of the volumes of the series are by the same author or authors, and the author has therefore been named in the catalog entry preceding the series note, the appropriate possessive pronoun is substituted for the author's name, unless the name is an integral part of the series title.

(*His* Wild world tales)

(*Her* Brontë sources, 2)

(*Their* The corridors of time, 8)

(*Its* Publications in research and records)

(Éditions de travail des œuvres de Schumann)

If a corporate body is considered to be the author of the series and not of the individual part being cataloged, the name of the corporate body is included in the series note as specified below.

1. The author of the series is included if author and title are integrated in the series statement.

(Neujahrsblatt der Allgemeinen Musikgesellschaft in Zürich)

(Historical publications of the Society of Colonial Wars in the Commonwealth of Pennsylvania)

(Contributions de l'Institut botanique de l'Université de Montréal, no. 61)

2. The author is included if it is essential to the identification of the series. The form of the series note is, in such a case, author in the form used for catalog entry, followed by the title. If, however, this form involves a language different from that of the series title or an author heading with more than one subdivision, the author statement is given in the form appearing on the work in any intelligible order, omitting any unessential part.

(Australia. Council for Scientific and Industrial Research. Bulletin no. 216)

([Gt. Brit. Foreign Office] Treaty series, 1948, no. 31)

(Kentucky. ₍State Geologist₎ Bulletin no. 20)

(Instituto de Geografía de la Universidad de Chile. Publicación no. 2)

(Université de Louvain. Collection de l'École des sciences politiques et sociales, no. 126)

(Universiteit te Leuven. Reeks van de School voor Economische Wetenschappen, nr. 26)

(U. S. Social Security Administration. Bureau of Research and Statistics. Bureau memorandum no. 69)

E. *Works in more than one series.* If a work is a part of more than one series, the second series note is placed, without parentheses but with brackets if necessary, as the first supplementary note. The series that is chosen for the first (regular) position is the one that is more specialized and less extensive, if such a comparison is possible. However, if one series title leaves no doubt as to its nature as a series and the other is not immediately recognizable as the title of a series, the latter is chosen for the regular position.

If the second series is a subordinate part of the first, the series and the subseries are specified in the same note. If the subseries has an author different from that of the main series, the subseries is treated as a second series.

(Biblioteca del lavoro. Serie professionale)

(Biblioteca de arte hispánico, 8. Artes aplicadas, 1)

(U. S. Dept. of State. Publication 1564. Executive agreement series, 94)

3:17. "AT HEAD OF TITLE" NOTE

A conventional note beginning with the phrase "At head of title" is generally used to note any essential information appearing in that position on the title page of the work unless the statement is transposed to another position in the catalog entry, as series, author statement, subtitle, edition, etc. Information noted in this fashion includes the names of corporate bodies whose relationship to the work as sponsor or issuing body is unknown or cannot be concisely stated, names of personal authors that cannot be simply transposed to the position following the title because case endings would be involved, statements that seem to be neither series nor subtitle, and any other information that is not provided for by the general pattern of the catalog entry.

a. *Different form of author's name from that in the heading.*

   Author's name in Chinese at head of title.

b. *Corporate body with subdivision not used in heading.*

   At head of title: Confederazione fascista degli agricoltori. Direzione sindacale. Ufficio studi legislativi.

   (*Entry: Confederazione fascista degli agricoltori.*)

c. *Corporate body not chosen as author heading although named at head of title.*

   At head of title: República de Chile. Armada Nacional.
   (*Entry: Chile. Laws, statutes, etc.*)

   At head of title: International Labour Organisation.
   (*Entry: International Labor Conference. 27th, Paris, 1945.*)

At head of title: Istituto di zootecnia della Università di Milano.
(*Entry: Piana, Giuseppe.*)

d. *Initials, seal or other insignia indicating the necessity for an added entry.*

Seal of State of Minnesota Forest Service at head of title.

e. *Miscellaneous types of data not included in the body of the entry.*

At head of title: Confidential.

At head of title: A Mr. and Mrs. North mystery.

At head of title: Germain Bazin, Jacques Combe, Michel Florisoone, René Huyghe, Charles Sterling.
(*Entry: Huyghe, René. La peinture française; la peinture actuelle.*)

At head of title: Junior high school, remedial reading.

At head of title: They came from Ireland.
(*Entry: Judson, Clara (Ingram) Michael's victory.*)

Title in Chinese precedes English title.

3:18. NOTES OF WORKS BOUND TOGETHER

If several works issued independently are subsequently bound together, the entry for each work in the volume bears a note to show the presence of the other work or works. For the first work in the volume, the note is simply a matter of physical description and need not have prominence. Since, also, it may not apply to other copies of the work, the note is generally the last one in the entry. For the second or any succeeding work in the volume, for which the note may be necessary to identify the work on the shelves or to explain a call number that appears to be incorrect, a prominent position is desirable; it is usually the first supplementary note.

The note begins:

> Bound with
> Bound with the author's [or authors']

If two or more distinct works, each with its own title page and paging, are issued together in one cover, the description is the same unless the cover is paper. The note then begins:

> With, as issued,

The citation of the other work or works in the volume, to be added to the above, takes the following form: the author's name in catalog entry form, with forenames (if more than one) represented by initials, brief title, place and date of publication, and size if it varies two or more centimeters from the size of the other work. If there are more than two titles bound together all are cited only in the entry for the first item in the work.

> Bound with the author's Out of the depths. [New York, 1945?] and Nash, Robert. Label your luggage. [New York, 1945?]
> Bound with the author's Our Lady's hours. [New York, 1945?]
> Bound with Ryan, Mary. Our Lady's hours. [New York, 1945?]

If the works bound together are numerous (such as a collection of pamphlets or other small works) or are to be classified as a collection, a collective catalog entry is prepared. If the parts are also to be cataloged separately, their place in the collection is indicated. The specification is given in a supplementary note in the analytical entry. (See Chapter 6, Analytical entries.)

> No. 3 in a vol. with binder's title: Brownist tracts, 1599-1644.
> Vol. 140, no. 6, of a collection with binder's title: Waterman pamphlets.

3:19. SEQUELS

A brief note in the form illustrated below is used to name a sequel to the work being cataloged or to name an earlier title which the work being cataloged continues, unless this information is shown by the subtitle.

> Sequel: Le collier de la reine.
> Sequel to Mémoires d'un médecin.

3:20. DISSERTATION NOTE

Academic dissertations presented in partial fulfillment of the requirements for a degree usually carry a formal statement, more or less uniform, depending upon the country of origin, naming the institution or faculty to which the dissertation was presented and the degree for which the author was a candidate. This statement is reduced to a brief, formal note giving the designation of the dissertation and the institution to which it was presented. If the author was a candidate for a degree other than that of doctor, this fact is also shown.

> Thesis (M.A.)—Johns Hopkins University.
> Tesis (licenciatura en derecho)—Universidad Nacional Autónoma de México.

A. *Designation of the dissertation.* The word "thesis" is used to designate any dissertation presented to obtain a degree at an institution in the United States. A foreign dissertation is designated by the term, or an abbreviation of the term, used on the work: thèse, proefschrift, akademisk avhandling, Inaugural-Dissertation, etc. If the work contains no specific designation, the word "thesis" is used.

Certain of the French universities require a "thèse" and a "thèse complémentaire." These are described, respectively, in the terms of the work, Thèse (1ʳᵉ) and Thèse (2ᵐᵉ) or Thèse complémentaire, unless the "deuxième thèse" referred to on the title page of the dissertation signifies the candidate's oral examination, in which case the number of the "first" one is not specified.

An abstract, abridgment, summary, or other portion of a thesis is described, as far as possible, by adding to the brief, formal note the qualifying term used in the publication. Works that merely originated in or are based on theses are not considered theses unless publication in this form is known to have been accepted as fulfilling requirements for the degree.

B. *The degree.* Degrees are represented by abbreviations. Authorities for the abbreviations are Webster's *New International Dictionary, Who's Who in America,* and the catalog of the institution granting the degree.

C. *The institution.* The name of the institution to which the dissertation was presented is named as briefly as possible. Most of the older and more famous continental universities are designated simply by the name of the place in which they are located (in the form adopted for author headings in the catalog). For French theses from 1808 to July 10, 1896, when the whole system of French education was centralized as the Université de France, with the former universities becoming local faculties, the name of the faculty rather than the university is used in the thesis note.

> Thesis—Yale.
> Thèse—Lyon.
> Inaug.-Diss.—Heidelberg.
> Promotionsarbeit—Eidgenössische Technische Hochschule, Zürich.

D. *Edited texts.* If the thesis is a text edited by the candidate, and therefore entered under its author or title rather than under the name of the candidate, the thesis note includes the name or designation of the editor.

> The editor's thesis—University of Chicago.
> Karl Schmidt's dissertation—Munich.

E. *Joint authors.* If the thesis is a work of joint authorship, the thesis note indicates which authors were candidates for degrees.

> The authors' thesis—Johns Hopkins University.
> R. V. Martin's thesis—Ohio State University.

F. *Praeses and respondent.* In an entry for a foreign dissertation in which designation of praeses and respondent is used, the name of the respondent (the candidate for the degree) is included in the thesis note.

> Diss.—Wittenberg (P. G. Scheibler, respondent)

G. *Latin theses.* If the candidate's name is included in the formal note for a Latin dissertation, the surname is given in the form used for the catalog entry and forenames are represented by initials.

H. *Theses without thesis statement.* The formal thesis note is used to describe a thesis even though it is issued without a thesis statement, if the information is available that the publication fulfilled the requirements of the university granting the degree. The absence of the thesis statement is noted.

> Thesis—Columbia University.
> Without thesis statement.

If some of the copies of such an edition without a thesis statement are designated as a thesis by means of a statement overprinted or stamped on the work, or by means of a mounted label or the addition of a special title page with the same title, the treatment is the same except that the nature of the thesis statement is explained.

> Thesis statement stamped on cover.

If, however, the additional title page, cover, or label bears a different title, the work is cataloged from the thesis title and note of the original form of publication is made.

> Halvorson, Halvor Orin, 1897–
>
> The importance of bacteria in the transformation of iron in nature. ₁Baltimore, 1931₁
>
> 141–165 p.   26 cm.
>
> Thesis—University of Minnesota.
> Thesis t. p., with Vita, mounted on p. ₁2₁ and ₁3₁ of cover.
> Cover title: Studies on the transformations of iron in nature: III.   The effect of CO_2 on the equilibrium in iron solutions.
> "Reprinted from Soil science, vol. XXXII, no. 2, August, 1931."

I. *Thesis and non-thesis editions.* If a work is issued in a thesis edition and also in a non-thesis edition, and all of the elements of the description with the exception of the thesis statement are the same, the two works are considered copies. (See 4:1.) If two catalog entries are necessary they are correlated by notes.

For thesis edition:

> Thesis—Columbia University.
> Published also without thesis statement.
>
> Thesis—Columbia University.
> Published also as Teachers College, Columbia University, Contributions to education, no. 724.

For non-thesis edition:

> Issued also as thesis, Columbia University.

J. *Vita.* A biographical sketch of the author accompanying his thesis is noted as "Vita" without page citation. If, however, the sketch is printed only on the cover, or on a label mounted on the work, the description is specific.

> Vita: p. ₁3₁ of cover.
> Vita on label mounted on last page.

3:21. "HABILITATIONSCHRIFTEN," "REKTORATSREDEN," "PRO-GRAMMSCHRIFTEN," ETC.

In cataloging treatises, addresses, and essays presented to European schools or institutions of higher learning as matter of routine or on special occasions, a formal note similar to that used in describing academic dissertations is used. The note is stated in the terms of the work as far as possible and gives the following information: the character of the work, the institution to which it was presented, and the occasion of the presentation if the work is not of a routine character.

> Habilitationschrift—Zürich.
> Rede—Tübingen (Geburtstag des Königs) 1915.

If it is issued with a "programm" this fact is shown.

> Accompanies "Programm" (Index scholarum sem. aest.)—Universität Greifswald.

> Accompanies "program" (Inbjudning till professorinstallation)—Lund.
> Separate from "Programm"—Gelehrtenschule des Johanneums, Hamburg.

If, however, the program is cataloged as an analytical entry for a serial publication that is entered under the name of the institution, the program note does not repeat the name of the institution.

> Tübingen. Universität. *Bibliothek*.
>
> Verzeichniss indischer Handschriften der Königlichen Universitäts-Bibliothek.
>
> (*In* Tübingen. Universität. Tübinger Universitätsschriften 1865. Tübingen, 1866. 25 cm. 24 p.)
>
> Accompanies "Programm" (Geburtsfest des Königs Karl von Württemberg)

3:22. CONTENTS NOTE

A. *Scope.* Either all of the contents or a part of them are specified in the catalog entry if it is necessary to bring out important parts of the work not mentioned in the title, or to give a fuller and more detailed description of the contents than the title supplies. If an added entry is to be made for an item in the work, the presence of this item is specified in the contents or partial contents note. The complete contents are listed in the entry for collections of works by the same author (especially if they are on different subjects) or for collections of works by different authors, unless the articles are numerous and slight or of the same type.

Contents are especially necessary for works in several volumes, whether they are single works (with a formal division of matter that can be described) or collections of works by one or more authors.

The contents of "Festschriften" are usually itemized, unless the note would be extremely long. Twenty-five contributions are usually the maximum listed.

Partial contents are noted if one or more selected items in the work need to be specified. Bibliographies are noted unless they are obviously of little value. Bibliographical footnotes are mentioned only if they seem to be particularly important or take the place of a bibliography that would have been noted. Appendices are noted only if they contain matter that is important enough to be specified. Errata, addenda, etc., are not noted if they are printed as part of the work but are mentioned if they are later additions and so likely to be wanting from some copies. Supplements or other appended matter not printed with the work are always noted. (See Chapter 5, Supplements, indexes, etc.)

B. *Position.* The contents note (because of its length and the fact that in an open entry it will have additions) is the last note in the catalog entry. If specific items are noted in addition to the "Contents" or "Partial contents" paragraph, they precede the latter, generally in the order of the items in the work.

C. *Form.* The specification of one or more items in a work consists of the precise heading of the item as it is found in the work (generally as a caption or

heading of the piece or in a table of contents), a quoted statement from the work, or a statement phrased by the cataloger. If one to three selected items are noted, the inclusive pagination of the items is generally specified, unless a single item described is scattered throughout the work. In other cases, the contents are arranged in one paragraph, beginning with the word "Contents" or the phrase "Partial contents." The items are given in the order in which they appear in the work. Except in works of one volume, the parts of the work are designated, the terms being those used in the work itself, except that arabic numerals are substituted for roman numerals unless both are required for clarity. If the parts are unnumbered, volume or part numbers are supplied. If the number of bibliographical volumes does not correspond with the number of physical volumes and the collation statement needs amplification, the number of physical volumes follows the titles in the contents.

For works of one volume, the items in a contents paragraph are separated by a dash; for works of more than one volume, the dash precedes the volume number and items within the volumes are punctuated as separate sentences.

Introductions described in the title are not mentioned again in the contents paragraph. Prefatory and similar unsigned matter is also omitted.

In listing works by different authors, the title precedes the name of the author, as indicated in the examples below, unless such a statement would require the cataloger to supply case endings to the names of the authors. In such cases, the author's name in inverted form precedes the title. Initials are used for one or more forenames. Brackets are not used to show that the word "by" and its equivalents have been supplied.

Paging is given in the contents paragraph only for bibliographies, and for a particular item that occupies a disproportionately large portion of the work. If given, it is cited within parentheses.

If the volumes of a set are of different editions, the editions and imprint dates are given in the contents paragraph.

Contents of a set in many volumes may be paragraphed, one paragraph to a volume, with "Contents" centered as heading. Contents of a collection of separately published pamphlets may be given in column form, with "Contents" centered as heading, the author's name given first in inverted form, and the imprint date added after each title.

D. *Examples.*

"Reading lists": p. 851–910.

"Selected bibliography": v. 1, p. 351–358; v. 2, p. 234–235.

Chronological list of the author's works: p. 469–475.

Includes bibliographies.

"Analytical digest of treaty provisions, by Herbert A. Smith": p. 159–216.

Appendices (p. 157–200): A. The Anglo-Japanese alliance.—B. The Russo-Japanese peace treaty.—C. The Japan-Korea agreement.

"Errata": 2 p. inserted.

Erratum slip mounted on p. 432.

PARTIAL CONTENTS.—Baptisms, 1816–1872.—Church members, 1816–1831.—History of the Second Presbyterian Church of West Durham, by L. H. Fellows.

CONTENTS.—How these records were discovered.—A short sketch of the Talmuds.—Constantine's letter ...

CONTENTS.—Introduction, by H. H. Brinton.—William I. Hull, a biographical sketch by J. Whitney.—George Fox as a man, by F. Aydelotte.—List of books by William Hull (p. 242)

CONTENTS.—Tartesso e a rota do estanho, por E. Simões de Paula.—Gadis, as navegações atlânticas e a rota das Índias na antiguidade, por J. Gagé.

CONTENTS.—v. 1. Plain tales from the hills.—v. 2–3. Soldiers three and military tales.—v. 4. Under the deodars. The story of the Gadsbys. Wee Willie Winkie.—v. 5. The phantom rickshaw and other stories.

CONTENTS.—t. 1. Dulce y sabrosa. 4. ed. 1921.—t. 2. La honorada. 3. ed. 1916.—t. 3. ...

CONTENTS.—₁1₁ Testo.—₁2₁ Tavole.

CONTENTS.

₁1₁ American Peace Society. Should the Unit d States of America join the Permanent Court of International Justice? 1931₁

₁2₁ Bustamente y Sirvén, A. S. de. The Wond Court and the United States. ₁1929₁

3:23. "TITLE TRANSLITERATED" NOTE

A note beginning "Title transliterated" is included in the entry for each work the title of which is in non-Latin characters. The words "Title transliterated" are italicized, followed by a colon and the title of the work in transliterated form according to the transliteration tables in the *A. L. A. Cataloging Rules for Author and Title Entries.* If the title is long, only the first part (preferably enough to stand alone) is transliterated. This note is printed in the lower right corner of the entry, following the tracing.

3:24. "FULL NAME" NOTE, ETC.

Certain author headings consisting of names of persons require amplification that can be supplied by a brief, conventional note, which (to separate it from the notes referring to the title of the work) is printed in the lower right corner of the catalog entry. If there is also a "Title transliterated" note the "name" note is given last. The most common note of this kind is the "full name" note which states the full form of a name for which an abridged form is used for the catalog entry.

The note begins with the phrase "Full name" (printed in italics) and a colon; this is followed by the name in normal order, including titles of nobility, etc., italicized according to the rules for entry. In languages such as Hungarian in which the family name is customarily given first, that order is used in the full name note.

If the author statement in the catalog entry gives the author's name in full, it is not repeated in a full name note.

Full name notes for married women who are still living are rarely used because of the difficulty of determining such names and of keeping them up to date.

Conventional notes similar to the full name note are made to show the real or original names of authors who are entered under their literary names, or who have legally changed their names; to show secular names of persons entered under a religious name and vice versa; to show stage names; to show real names of authors who have written jointly under a single pseudonym, etc.

> *Full name:* Francis Bret Harte.
>
> *Full name:* Friedrich Wilhelm Heinrich Alexander *Freiherr* von Humboldt.
>
> *Real name:* Louis Farigoule.
>
> *Real name* (*reputedly*): Leo Noussimbaum.
>
> *Name originally:* Ford Madox Hueffer.
>
> *Name in religion:* Mary Bartholomew, *Sister.*
>
> *Secular name:* Katharine Mary Brosnahan.
>
> *Stage name of* Leslie Townes Hope.
>
> Ellery Queen, *pseud. of* Frederic Dannay *and* Manfred Bennington Lee.
>
> Ted Malone, *pseud. of* Frank Alden Russell.
>> (*This explanation of the pseudonym used by a single individual is used only if the pseudonym in the author statement is in the possessive case, as Ted Malone's Album of poetic shrines.*)
>
> *Full name:* Johann August Wilhelm Neander. (*Original name:* David Mendel)

3:25. TRACING OF SECONDARY ENTRIES

Each catalog entry includes a record, or "tracing, " of all of the secondary entries that are to be made for the work. These include the entries under subject headings, entries for joint authors, editors, translators, and others who have had a significant part in or responsibility for the work, an entry for the title if it will be useful for finding the work, an entry for an alternative or partial title if the work is likely to be known by it, and entry for the series if an approach under the name of the series is to be provided for the work.

This record is added to the catalog entry following all of the notes, in a single paragraph. The subject headings are listed first, numbered consecutively with arabic numerals, followed by the other secondary entries, numbered with roman numerals except for the series entry which is unnumbered and enclosed in parentheses. If there are several added entries for persons or corporate bodies, they are listed in the order in which they appear in the catalog entry, except that all entries for persons generally precede the entries for corporate bodies. Added entries for title entry, the partial title if such entry is to be made, and for the series follow in this order. Each is traced to show the form in which it is to be found in the catalog. Unless the title is to be found as it appears in the catalog entry, the word "Title" in the tracing is followed by the selected form of the title.

> 1. Title: Employee manual.

If the series is entered as it appears in the series note, only the word "Series" is given in the tracing. Any variation between the series note and the series entry is shown.

> *Note:* (Veröffentlichungen der Schleswig-holsteinischen Universitäts-Gesellschaft, Nr· 43)
>
> *Tracing:* (Series: Schleswig-holsteinische Universitäts-Gesellschaft. Veröffentlichungen, Nr. 43)
>
> *Note:* (S. P. E. tract no. 36)
>
> *Tracing:* (Series: Society for Pure English. Tract no. 36)

If a second series (or the first series if for any reason it is not given in the customary position following the collation) is traced, its catalog entry is always specified. If several volumes, or parts of the series, that are not consecutively numbered are included in the series note, only the first, followed by "₍etc.₎" is included in the tracing.

4. Issues, Offprints, etc.

4:1. ISSUES

The various issues of a given edition may be cataloged as copies, as different issues, or as different editions. (See 3:1 A.) Issues treated as copies are noted, with variations other than a different imprint date or change in the form of the name of the publisher being specified. Two dashes (the first, 2 ems, the second, 3 ems in length) are added to the catalog entry for the first one received, followed by the copy number and note of the variation.

—— ——Copy 2. Without thesis statement.

If variations between issues are so great that the publications cannot be treated as copies but the title and text of the works are the same, they are cataloged as different issues. Two dashes, as for copies, are added, followed by the phrase "Another issue" and the specification of bibliographical details which differentiate the issue received later.

—— ——Another issue.
30 cm. Large paper ed.
—— ——Another issue.
104 p. (p. 101–104 advertising matter)

4:2. OFFPRINTS

An offprint, or separate, of an article, chapter or other portion of a larger work is cataloged as an independent monograph if the larger work is not in the Library's collections. The relationship to the larger work is specified.

If the larger work is in the Library, an analytical entry is prepared for the part represented by the offprint and the latter is described with a "dash" entry as explained in the second paragraph of 4:1. (See also Chapter 6, Analytical entries.)

—— ——Offprint.
Cover dated 1946.

4:3. DETACHED COPIES OF PARTS OF WORKS

A part of a work detached from a copy of the work as a whole, in order to be classified as a separate work or for other reason, is cataloged as if it were bibliographically independent; the resulting entry is not an analytical entry. An explanatory note is added to the catalog entry.

Davis, *Sir* **John Francis,** *bart.,* 1795–1890.

Poeseos Sinensis commentarii. On the poetry of the Chinese. Read May 2, 1829. ₍London, 1830₎

393–461 p. 29 cm.

Detached from Transactions of the Royal Asiatic Society of Great Britain and Ireland, v. 2.

If, however, the Library has a copy of the larger work as well as the detached copy, the analytical entry is prepared for the former and the latter is noted as a second copy.

—— ———Copy 2, detached.

44

5. Supplements, Indexes, etc.

5:1. ENTRY WITH MAIN WORK

Continuations of, and supplements and indexes to, monographic publications that are not independent of the work to which they belong are described in the entry for the main work.

If they are minor in character, they may simply be noted informally.

"Tables I, II, and III omitted by error from report" published as suppl. (5 p.) and inserted at end.

"Armorial général de France. Table des noms inscrits dans ce recueil" issued as special suppl. with v. 9–14 (1863–69)

If contents are given for the main work, the supplementary volumes may be included as part of the contents statement, even though they are not numbered consecutively with the other volumes.

... v. 10. Southern California. Grand Cañon of the Colorado River. Yellowstone National Park.—Supplementary volumes: [no. 1] Ireland (two lectures) Denmark. Sweden. no. 2. Canada (two lectures) Malta. Gibraltar.

... 5. 1705–1708.—6. 1709–1722.—7. General index.

If, however, a more complete description of the supplement is required, the following form is used: a dash (2 ems in length) to represent the repetition of the author heading, is added to the catalog entry following all of the paragraphed notes relating to the main work, but preceding the tracing. It is followed by the title of the supplement or index, the author statement (if necessary to show the compiler or other person responsible for the work), the edition statement, imprint, collation, etc., as for an independent work.

Carrier, Auguste Alexandre.

Traité de topographie générale (cours professé à l'École nationale du génie rural) Paris, Girard et Barrère, 1942.

580 p. illus., maps. 24 cm.

CONTENTS.—Éléments de géodésie.—Topographie.

——Astronomie topographique. Complément au Traité de topographie générale. Éd. provisoire. Paris, Girard et Barrère, 1943.

80 p. illus. 24 cm.

If the title of the supplement or index includes the title of the main work and can be separated from it, the title of the main work is represented by a second (3 em) dash, following the dash that represents the author.

Walpole, Horace, *earl of Orford,* 1717–1797.

The letters of Horace Walpole, fourth earl of Orford; chronologically arranged and edited with notes and indices by Mrs. Paget Toynbee.   Oxford, Clarendon Press, 1903–05.

16 v.   58 ports.   20 cm.

———— ————Supplement; chronologically arranged and edited with notes and indices by Paget Toynbee.   Oxford, Clarendon Press, 1918–25.

3 v.   ports., 2 fold. facsims.   20 cm.

5:2. INDEPENDENT ENTRY

A continuation or supplement that is in the form of an independent work, with author and title differing from that of the original work, is described according to the rules for cataloging independent monographic publications.

Copinger, Walter Arthur, 1847–1910.

Supplement to Hain's Repertorium bibliographicum. Or, Collections towards a new edition of that work.

Austin, Bryson Edward, 1851–1903.

The story of a New England farm house.   Boston, Ellis & Little, 1883.

106 p.   24 cm.

Issued as a suppl. to Massachusetts magazine of historical research, v. 12, no. 3.

6. Analytical Entries

6:1. DEFINITION. SCOPE

An analytical entry is an entry for a part of a work or series of works for which another, comprehensive, entry is made. The part analyzed may be a complete volume, bibliographically independent from the set of which it forms a part, or it may be a mere page or two which is inadequately described (either from the author or the subject approach) by the catalog entry for the work as a whole. If the part analyzed is an independent work, it is cataloged according to the rules for separately published monographs, with a series note indicating its relationship to the more comprehensive work. The rules in this chapter are limited to analytical entries for parts not bibliographically independent. These entries are commonly called "page" analyticals or "in" analyticals.

6:2. TYPES OF ANALYTICAL ENTRIES

A. *Parts with special title pages and separate paging.* If the part to be analyzed has a special title page, the body of the entry is prepared according to the rules for separate monographic publications. If it has also separate paging, the form of the collation corresponds also to that for separate monographic publications. The collation is followed (in the position otherwise occupied by the name of the series to which a work belongs) by a note showing the relationship of the part to the larger work. This "analytical" note is enclosed in parentheses, begins with the italicized word "In," and specifies the author (in catalog entry order but with initials substituted for forenames if there is more than one), brief title, edition, place and date of publication of the larger work. If the part to be analyzed forms the whole number of a series, this fact is shown in the first supplementary note.

> Frey, Janus Caecilius₎ *d.* 1631.
>
> Flöia, cortvm versicale, De Flôis schwartibus, illis deiriçulis, quæ omnes ferè Minachos, Mannos, Vveibras, Iungfras, &c. behùppere, & spitzibus suis schnaflis steckere & bitere solent. Authore Gripholdo Knickknackio ex Floilandia [pseud. n. p.] Anno 1593.
>
> ₍12₎ p. 20 cm. (*In* Blümlein, Carl, ed. Die Floia und andere deutsche maccaronische Gedichte. Strassburg, 1900)
>
> Drucke und Holzschnitte des XV. und XVI Jahrhunderts in getreuer Nachbildurg, 4.

If the larger work is in more than one volume, the number of the particular volume analyzed is added after the imprint, followed, in parentheses, by the date of the volume, unless it is the same as that of the larger work. If the larger work is still being published, its imprint dates are omitted.

> (*In* Harleian miscellany. London, 1808–13. v. 3 (1809))

B. *Parts with separate title pages and continuous paging.* If the part is paged continuously with other matter in the same volume, the analytical note is given in the position otherwise occupied by the collation. It agrees in form with the other analytical note except that the size of the volume, the inclusive pagination, or volume number and pagination, and the important illustrative matter of the part, are added after the imprint, in the order mentioned.

> Flaminiani,
> Ethelinda. An English novel done from the Italian. London, 1729.
>
> (*In* Croxall, Samuel, comp. **A select collection of novels and histories.** 2d ed. London, 1729. 17 cm. v. 5, p. ₁79₁–124)

C. *Parts without special title pages.* If the part to be analyzed does not have a special title page, the entry is prepared as in B above, except that the body of the entry consists only of the title of the part, followed by the author statement if one is necessary.

> Richardson, Henry Gerald, 1884–
> The morrow of the Great charter: an addendum.
>
> (*In* John Rylands Library, Manchester. Bulletin. Manchester. 27 cm. v. 29 (1945) p. 184–200)

D. *Analytical entries for parts of analyzed parts.* If an analytical entry is required for a part of a work which is itself cataloged by means of an analytical entry, two analytical notes are necessary. The first note refers to the comprehensive work (because this information may be necessary to locate the work on the shelves and to explain the call number), the second note refers to the lesser work in which the part is contained.

6:3. UNIT CARDS AS ANALYTICAL ENTRIES

If the catalog entry for a work includes (in title, contents or other place) reference to a part for which analytical entry is required, an added entry may be made instead of a separate analytical entry.

> Smith, Alfred Emanuel, 1873–1944.
> Addresses delivered at the meetings of the Society of the Friendly Sons of St. Patrick, 1922–1944 ... ₁New York₁ Society of the Friendly Sons of St. Patrick in the City of New York, 1945.
>
> 129 p. port., col. facsim. 24 cm.
> "Address of Honorable James A. Foley": p. 4–19.
> I. Foley, James A., 1882–1946. II. Society ...

If the part has been, or is likely to be, published separately or referred to by its title, the added entry takes the form of the author and title of the part.

Chittenden, Richard Handy.
Verse and prose. Brooklyn, H. M. Gardner, Jr., printer,
1879–81.

386 p. 24 cm.

Includes translations from Faust.

i. Goethe, Johann Wolfgang von. Faust.

If, however, the added entries would be so numerous that the tracing would be
cumbersome, analytical entries are preferred. Likewise, if the part to be analyzed
requires its own secondary entries other than title, such as subject headings, name
of translator, etc., the special analytical entries may be necessary.

7. Serials

7:1. SCOPE OF THESE RULES

The general principles for cataloging serials are the same as those for cataloging monographic publications; wherever suitable, the rules for the cataloging of monographs are to be applied to serials. However, the fact that one catalog entry must record the bibliographical history of a sequence of many individual parts which undergo numerous changes during the course of publication necessarily gives rise to special rules to supplement the others. It is essential to record such information as variation in titles, changes of name of issuing bodies, connection with preceding or succeeding publications, and statement of indexes, to mention only the more important. These items are condensed, tabulated, and recorded in a form in which no essential fact is lost, although the exact wording of title pages is shown less frequently than in the cataloging of monographs. The aim is to prepare an entry that will stand the longest time and will permit the making of necessary changes with the minimum of modification.

Whether a serial is monographic (i. e., a series) or not does not affect its cataloging although it may affect its classification, since the separate parts of a series may be classified separately while those of a non-monographic serial must be classified together. For this reason, no special rules for the description of series are necessary, the rules for serials as a whole being applicable. Because of the practical difficulties involved in keeping up to date the card for a set that is not kept together on the shelves, the Library of Congress does not generally make a main entry for series of which volumes are classified separately. For important series the unit card for each volume is filed in the catalog under the name of the series.

Certain types of publications, perhaps properly called continuations, are cataloged according to the rules for cataloging serials. These publications include works which are issued frequently in new editions (such as certain who's whos, guidebooks, etc.) even though they may be works of personal authorship.

7:2. VARIATIONS FROM THE CATALOGING OF MONOGRAPHIC PUBLICATIONS

The rules in this chapter show the application of the general rules to the cataloging of serial publications and provide additional rules as necessary. The chief differences in the form of the catalog entry for a serial from that for a monograph may be summarized as follows:

a. A serial publication in several volumes with varying bibliographical details is described from the latest volume, with the variations from that volume noted, whereas a monographic work in several volumes is cataloged from the first volume, with variations noted.

b. The editor statement is given as a supplementary note instead of in the body of the entry, because the more prominent position following the title is devoted to the statement of "holdings" and because, when editors change, the adding of that information is more convenient and economical if the editor statement has been given in a note.

c. The catalog entry for a serial publication should show the record of the volumes published and indicate which ones are in the Library's collections or should refer to a listing of such volumes.[1]

d. An important feature for the characterization of a serial, and occasionally for its identification, is the frequency of its publication.

e. If the statement of holdings does not show the duration of publication, supplementary notes are essential to show it. This includes the facts of suspension and resumption of publication.

f. The fact that a serial is the organ of a society or other body must be stated.

g. Serial publications frequently have special numbers that must be described.

7:3. SOURCE OF DATA FOR BODY OF ENTRY

The data given in the body of the entry, with the exception of the record of holdings, are taken from a single source as far as possible. If the publication has no title page, the title is taken from the cover, caption, masthead, editorial pages or other place, the order of preference being that of this listing. The source of the data is specified if it is not the title page, cover, caption or masthead. However, if there is no title page and the cover, caption or other titles differ, the source of the title used is specified and the other titles noted.

The title page, or title page substitute, chosen as the basis of the catalog entry is that of the latest volume, so that the latest title and corresponding imprint are given the prominence of the body of the entry. Earlier forms are noted as variations. Exception to this rule is made in the case of a serial which has ceased publication, if an earlier title has continued for a much longer period of time than the later title. In such a case the title chosen for the body of the entry is the one that persisted the longest.

7:4. THE RECORDING OF THE TITLE

A short title is generally used in cataloging serial publications if this makes it possible to disregard minor variations in the wording on various issues, especially

---

[1] The Library of Congress uses a rubber stamp reading "Apply for volume desired" on each card which does not list the Library's holdings. Other libraries using these cards will also have to add such a note or refer the user to another catalog such as the shelf list or a special record of serials, or supplement the printed cards with a manuscript or typewritten record of holdings.

if these occur in subtitles. Subtitles are omitted unless necessary for identification or for clarification of the scope of the publication. Adjectives denoting the frequency of the publication are also omitted (without mark of omission) from the titles of reports; e. g., *Report* instead of *Annual report* and *Biennial report, Financial statement* instead of *Monthly financial statement*, etc.

If a number appearing as part of the title is considered to be the volume designation it is omitted from the title (without mark of omission); e.g., *Report of the first annual meeting* becomes *Report of the annual meeting*.

7:5. HOLDINGS

The statement of the volumes "held" by the Library is given immediately after the title or subtitle in the catalog entry. If the work has ceased publication but the Library does not have all of the volumes that have been published, the extent of the complete set is recorded, provided the information is available;[2] the volumes that are lacking are specified in a supplementary note. If essential data are not available, the statement of holdings consists only of the data relating to the first issue. If information about the first issue is not available, no record of holdings is given.

If a serial is still in progress of publication, or if the final issue has been published but reliable information as to its number or date of issue is not available, the statement of holdings consists only of the data relating to the first issue.

A. *Scope.* The statement of holdings records the volume designation or the date of issue or both. The date may consist of the month, day and year; month or season and year; or year alone, depending upon the frequency of publication and the usage of the publisher. The statement is limited to volume designation for those publications that do not carry dates by which the parts are identified; volume designation may be a volume number, edition number, or other designation according to the usage of the publisher.

B. *Abbreviations and numerals.* Abbreviations for terms used in volume designations and for months are given in the vernacular. Arabic numerals are used. (See Appendix III.)

C. *Punctuation.* Volume, report, and edition numbers are separated from the dates by a semicolon. If there are two or more series of volume numbers, commas are used between volumes and dates, and semicolons between series. Whole numbers, i.e., the numbers of parts which continue from one volume to another, are enclosed in parentheses following the volume numbers.

Housing index-digest. v. [1]–4, no. 3; June 15, 1936–Nov. 1, 1940.

---

[2] The chief sources of this information are the National Union Catalog and the *Union List of Serials.* The extent of the complete set need not be recorded if the Library's holdings are very fragmentary.

Continente; revista internacional.   año 1–4 (núm. 1–48); set.
   1941–agosto 1944.

Archives des sciences physiques et naturelles.   t. 1–36, 1846–
   57; nouv. période, t. 1–64, 1858–78; 3. période, t. 1–34,
   1879–95; 4. période, t. 1–46, 1896–1918; 5. période, t. 1–
   1919–

Sindicato nazionale fascista ingegneri.
   Annuario.   1.–4. ed.; 1920–24.

Aviation equipment red book.   1944–   ed.

A hyphen is used in recording the date of a report that covers two or more
calendar years.   A diagonal line between two dates is used to indicate a year that
is not a calendar year.   A hyphen connects the dates of the first and the final
issue unless one of them contains a hyphen; in this case a dash is used to connect
the dates of the first and the final issue.

U. S. *Bureau of Reclamation.*
   Report.   1st–14th; 1902–1914/15.

Montana's production; a statistical summary of the state's
   industries.   1930–38—

The data in the statement of holdings are not enclosed in brackets when ascertainable from the issue being cataloged even though they do not appear on the
title page or title page substitute which forms the basis of the catalog entry.
Brackets are not used to enclose the "v." or comparable designation if it appears
in a later volume of the publication.

7:6. IMPRINT

The imprint in the catalog entry for a serial publication is limited to the place
of publication and the name of the publisher if dates are recorded in the statement
of holdings following the title.   (See also 3:10–3:13.)
   If the record of the final volume is not included in the statement of holdings, the
imprint begins a new line in the catalog entry.

A. *Place of publication.*   Changes in the place of publication that do not warrant
specific description are indicated by the abbreviation "etc." following the place of
publication.   (See 7:8 L.)   If the name of the place has changed during the course
of publication of the work being cataloged, the earlier form of name is added,
within parentheses, after the later form; e.g., Oslo (Christiania).

B. *Publisher.*   If the name of the publisher is essentially the same as the title
of the publication, as is often the case with periodicals, it is omitted from the
imprint.
   Minor changes in the name of the publisher as it appears on the various volumes,
and changes of publisher not warranting specific description, are indicated in the
imprint by the use of "etc." after the name of the publisher.   (See 7:8 L.)

7:7. COLLATION

The collation statement is prepared as far as possible to describe the completed set. If the Library does not have a complete set and if the information is easily ascertained, the total number of volumes is indicated. Illustrative matter is described for the set as a whole.

A. *Volumes.* The statement of the number of volumes is left open until the serial has ceased publication and the total number of volumes or the pagination can be recorded. (See 3:14 B.)

B. *Numbers.* If the parts of a serial are described as numbers in the publication and there is no comprehensive volume numbering, they are designated as "no." in the collation. If they are bound together, the number of volumes is also given.

> 25 no. in 3 v.

C. *Pagination.* The pagination of a serial that is complete in one volume is recorded according to the rules for describing the pagination of separately published monographs. (See 3:14 A.)

D. *Illustrations.* Only those types of illustration that are, or probably are, important to the set as a whole are included in the description of a serial publication. A single illustration of a given type (map, plan, port., etc.) is always ignored. (See also 2.14 C.)

E. *Size.* See 3:14 D. Variations in the width of serial publications are ignored.

7:8. NOTES

Many of the supplementary notes necessary to the cataloging of serial publications are presented in a conventional style. Although the circumstances of the case must necessarily govern the phrasing of any note, the following paragraphs indicate what types of information are essential, and suggest forms. At times unnecessary repetition can be avoided, without sacrifice of clarity, by combining two or more conventional or other notes.

In describing bibliographical changes in a serial publication, reference is generally made to the date of the volume or issue showing the change rather than to its volume designation, unless the date of the volume or issue is not sufficient and volume designation must be used. Dates, and the designation of volumes when used (except in contents notes) are given in English, with appropriate abbreviations, unless the vernacular is essential to clarity. Dates may be described by the month, day and year, by the month or season and year, or by year alone, as the situation may require. If any change described in a note occurs with the first issue in the month, the day is not specified; if it occurs with the first issue in the year, the month or season is not specified.

In general, the order of the items below is observed in the catalog entry.

A. *Frequency.* If the frequency of publication can be described by a single adjective or brief phrase, it is given immediately after the collation, unless it is obvious from the title of the publication; e. g., *Quarterly journal of current acquisitions.*

> v.   illus.   21 cm.   annual.
> v.   illus.   21 cm.   3 no. a year.
> v.   illus.   21 cm.   monthly (except July and Aug.)
> v.   illus.   21 cm.   semimonthly (during the school year)

This conventional form of note is not used if a more extended statement is necessary. For example:

> Issued several times a week.
> Monthly, accompanied by a midmonthly supplement.
> Four no. a year, 1931; 5 no. a year, 1932–34.
> Monthly, 1901–June 1904; quarterly, Sept. 1904.

If there are numerous changes in frequency of publication, the information is omitted or represented by the general note, "Frequency varies."

B. *Report year.* If the period covered by an annual report is other than that of the calendar year, the fact is noted.

> Report year ends June 30.
> Report year irregular.
> Report year for 1928–30 ends June 30; for 1931–34, Dec. 31.

The period covered by reports other than annual is noted if possible.

> Period covered by report ends Mar. 31.
> Period covered by reports is irregular.
> Fourth report covers period Mar. 1942–Dec. 1943.

C. *Duration of publication.* The duration of publication is stated in a note, unless it is shown by the statement of holdings. The note position for this information is preferred to inclusion in the body of the entry if the authenticity of the data is questioned or if the details regarding volumes and dates are not available.

> Began publication with Apr. 1943 issue.   Cf. Willing's press guide.
> "Published ... since 1909."
> Ceased publication with v. 4, no. 4 (Aug. 1935?)   Cf. Union list of serials.
> Published 1820–64.   Cf. Union list of serials.

D. *Suspension of publication.* If a serial suspends publication with the intention of resuming at a later date, the entry is left open and a note is used to show date, or the volume designation, of the last issue published. If publication is resumed, the note shows the inclusive dates of the period of suspension.

> Publication suspended with v. 11.
> Publication suspended with Dec. 1942.
> Publication suspended 1923–31.
> Publication suspended during 1919.

56

E. *Numbering.* Irregularities and peculiarities in the numbering of a serial publication are described, unless they are limited to the numbers within, or parts of, a given volume. These include double numbering, confusion in the use of series numbering or whole numbers, the publication of preliminary editions not included in the regular series numbering, numbering that does not begin with volume one, etc.

> Issues for 1892–1902 called v. 2–12; 1903–April 1906 called v. 1–4, no. 4; May 1906–July 1910 called v. 1–5, no. 3.
> Issues for Feb.–Mar. 1939 have no vol. numbering but constitute v. 1, no. 1–2.
> Vol. numbers irregular: v. 15–18 omitted; v. 20–21 repeated.
> Vols. 13–36 called also "neue Folge," v. 1–24; v. 37– called also "2. Folge," v. 1–
> Second to fifth reports combined in one issue.
> Vols. 3–4 issued together.
> Vol. 1, no. 1 preceded by a number dated Jan. 12, 1940, called Sample copy.
> An introductory number was issued Nov. 30, 1935, called v. 1, no. 0.
> Vols. 1–7 not published.
> Formed by the union of "Spirits" and the "American wine and liquor journal" and assumed the vol. numbering of the latter.
> Supersedes, in part, Archivo español de arte y arqueología, and continues its vol. numbering.

F. *Connection with preceding publications.* Continuity between a serial and its predecessor or predecessors is indicated.

> Supersedes the Tropical veterinary bulletin.
> Supersedes an earlier publication with the same title, issued 1919–36.
> Began publication in May 1935, superseding the federation's Bulletin.
> Supersedes the Bibliographer (Dec. 1881–Nov. 1889) and Book-lore (Dec. 1884–Nov. 1887)
> Supersedes the Half-yearly abstract of the medical sciences, published in Philadelphia.
> Published during the suspension of Book-plate booklet.

G. *Organ.* The fact that a serial is the organ of a society or other body is presented in the terms, or the English equivalents of the terms, used by the publisher, unless the fact is obvious from the author entry of the work.

> Official organ of the Interne Council of America, 1938–41; journal of the Association of Internes and Medical Students, 1942–
> Official journal of the Concrete Products Association, Oct. 1920–Apr. 1930.
> Organ of the Association provinciale des secrétaires de municipalités.
> Official medium of the International Association of Liberal Physicians (formerly National Association of Drugless Physicians) Dec. 1939–
> Official publication of the Peace Officers Civil Service Association of California and, 1930–37, of the California Academy of Police Science.
> Journal of the Minnesota State Medical Association and of other medical societies of Minnesota.

H. *Variations in title.* Changes in the title of the several volumes or parts of a serial publication so slight that they do not affect the location of the title in an alphabetical file, or conceal the identification of the parts, are mentioned in a general statement such as "Title varies slightly" or "Subtitle varies." Other changes are specified and the corresponding dates or volumes shown.

To note one or more changes in title, a conventional "title varies" note is generally used. Under this caption are shown all the important changes in title except the last, with the inclusive dates or volume designation or both, for the issues having each title. Slight variations in title within any given period may be shown by the phrase "varies slightly" in parentheses at the end of the statement.

> Title varies: 1891, New Zealand post and telegraph gazette.—1892–1902, The Katipo; a journal of events in connection with and circulated only in the New Zealand post office and telegraph service (subtitle varies slightly)—1903–Apr. 1906, The New Zealand post and telegraph officers' advocate.
>
> Title varies; v. 1–8, James Sprunt historical monograph.—v. 9–18, The James Sprunt historical publications.—v. 19–22, The James Sprunt historical studies.
>
> Title varies: Nov. 1921–Oct. 1924, Practical electrics.—Nov. 1924–Feb. 1926, The Experimenter; electricity, radio, chemistry.
>
> Title varies; Feb. 1903–Jan. 1905, The Lamp.

The varying forms of a title used on different parts of the publication are recorded in the catalog entry if they contribute to the identification of the publication.

> Binder's title, 1930–   : Anuario Córdoba.
> Cover title, July 1920–   : The Flame.
> Running title, 1940–Jan./Feb. 1942: The Canadian Red Cross dispatch.
> Title varies: Sept. 1934–Dec. 1936, The American Welding Society journal (running title: The Welding journal)—Jan. 1937–   The Welding journal; the journal of the American Welding Society (caption title: The American Welding Society journal)

If the varying form of the title appears on all volumes of a work that has ceased publication, the inclusive dates are unnecessary in the specification.

The presence of special titles of individual issues or volumes is mentioned in the catalog entry, the various titles being specified, if the individual volume is likely to be known by the special title.

> Each vol. has also a distinctive title: 1939, Government, the citizen's business.—1940, Explorations in citizenship.—1941, Self-government under war pressure.

I. *Variations in author's name and changes in authorship.* If a serial publication of a corporate body is continued by another corporate body, or by the same body with a changed name, it is necessary for the identification of the volumes to describe the variations. Inclusive dates, or volume designation of the issues published during the period of the variation, are included.

> Issued 1920–June 1933 by Babson's Statistical Organization, inc.
> Report for 1845 issued by the society under its earlier name: Foreningen for norske fortidsmindesmaerkers bevaring.

J. *Issuing bodies.* If the statement of issuing or sponsoring body or bodies is complex, if the name of another body appears as the publisher, if there are

changes in the name of the issuing body, or if there is more than one successive issuing body, the necessary information is added in a supplementary note.

> Issued 1925–Jan. 1933 under the auspices of the New Mexico State
> Highway Dept. (with the Dept. of Game and Fish, July 1931–Jan. 1933)
>
> Vol. 1 published by the students of the Claremont Colleges and La Verne
> College; v. 2–   by the students of Pomona College.
>
> Published by Kölner Bezirksverein Deutscher Ingenieure, Elektrotech-
> nische Gesellschaft zu Köln, and Architekten- und Ingenieurverein für
> Niederrhein und Westfalen.
>
> Published 1927–29 by the National Motor Bus Division (called in 1927,
> Bus Division; in 1928, Motor Bus Division) of the American Automobile
> Association; 1930–   by the National Association of Motor Bus Opera-
> tors, affiliated with the American Automobile Association.
>
> Published by the Westinghouse Club (formerly the Electric Club)

K. *Editors.* Unless a serial has ceased publication and has had the **same editor**
or group of editors throughout its life, the editors, compilers, directors **or founders**
who are important to the identification or characterization of the work **are named**
in a conventional note. (Editors for whom added entries are not to be made **are**
not noted.) The following are considered to have such importance:

1. Persons whose names are likely to be better known in relation **to the work**
than the exact title of the work itself.

2. Persons who have been associated with a publication (except **minor works**,
such as house organs, student publications, etc.) throughout the lifetime **of the**
serial or for a notably long period.

3. Persons who are responsible for a serial publication, other than **a periodical**,
that is published by a commercial firm without the direction of a society or other
body.

The conventional note begins with the word "Editor" or "Compiler," or other
appropriate designation, and shows the inclusive dates of the contribution of each
person named.

> Editor: 1939–   H. L. Mencken.
>
> Editors: 1894–1926, A. Sauer (with J. Nadler, 1914–26, G. Stefansky,
> 1926)—1927–31, J. Nadler, G. Stefansky and others.—1932–33, G.
> Stefansky and others.—1934–   H. Pongs (with J. Petersen, 1934–38)

An informal statement is preferred to a conventional note in cataloging a work
that has ceased publication and has had the same editor or group of editors
throughout, or if an informal statement is more satisfactory for other reasons.

> Ed. by A. Alonso.
>
> Founded and for some years ed. by O. Janke.

L. *Variations in imprint.* Variations in the place of publication and **changes**
of publisher are shown in conventional or informal notes as the circumstances **may**
require. A conventional note beginning with the phrase "Imprint varies" **is**
generally used unless there has been but one change of place and publisher. **An**
informal statement is used if the change is that of only the place or of the publisher,
or if the change consists of an important variation in the name of the publisher.

> Imprint varies: 1922–Oct. 1937, Chicago, Trade Union Educational League ·etc.¡—Nov. 1937–Mar. 1945, New York, Communist Party of the United States of America.
>
> Imprint varies: 1870–81, Leipzig, L. Voss.—1882–96, Hamburg, L. Voss.—1897–1920, Berlin, R. Friedlander.
>
> Imprint varies: 1827/1931, Cambridge, Harvard University Press.—1932/34, Chapel Hill, The University of North Carolina Press.
>
> Published in Leipzig, Sept. 1898–1930; in Hamburg, 1931–40.
>
> Vol. 3, no. 2, published by J. Debrett.
>
> Published in Rotterdam by Nijgh & Van Ditman, 1916–40.
>
> Vols. 1–3, no. 2, published under the foundation's earlier name: Research Foundation of Armour Institute of Technology.

M. *Titles absorbed.* The continuity of two or more serial publications is recorded by indicating that one serial has been absorbed by another. The title absorbed is named and the exact date of the absorption indicated if it can be determined.

> Absorbed the Philadelphia medical journal, June 20, 1903; Medical news, Jan. 6, 1906; Medical record, May 3, 1922; Medical herald, Feb. 7, 1934; Medical mentor, Mar. 7, 1934.
>
> Absorbed the Proceedings of the Pacific Northwest Library Association in Oct. 1937 and became the association's official organ.
>
> "Incorporating the Journeymen bakers' magazine."

N. *Mergers, unions, etc.* If a serial has merged into, united with, or been superseded by, another publication, this fact is noted. If the Library's holdings are not complete or if the merger does not follow immediately after the publication of the last issue, the date of the action is indicated.

> Absorbed by Monumental news-review.
>
> Superseded by a later publication with the same title.
>
> Merged into New York medical journal (later Medical record)
>
> Merged into Rock products in Dec. 1936.
>
> Superseded by Wille und Macht in Dec. 1936.
>
> United with the Home mission herald in Nov. 1911 to form the Missionary survey.
>
> Superseded by the Biological bulletin and indexed with v. 1–60 of that bulletin.
>
> Superseded by the Aeronautical review section of the Journal of the aeronautical sciences.

O. *"No more published?"* A note reading "No more published?" is added as the last note before the contents, if there is doubt as to whether or not the number designated as the last issue was in fact the final issue.

P. *Contents.* Contents are not specified in the catalog entries for serials that consist of a sequence of monographs that are, or may be, analyzed or that are relatively unimportant. Analyzed parts are represented by unit cards under the name of the series.

Notes concerning the inclusion of other serials in the contents are used to characterize the work as a whole, to indicate parts that are necessary for the

completeness of the volumes, and to specify special items that are important enough to warrant added entries.

Includes Federal regulation of exchanges, stock markets, corporation reports, margins, commodity exchanges, and cotton exchanges.

Vols. 26– issued in 3 sections: Aufsatzteil, Referatenteil, and Wirtschaftlicher Teil und Vereinsnachrichten.

Issues for 1946– include sections: Books, periodicals and films, and Who's who in industrial research.

Includes "Bibliography of Northwest materials."

Issues for 1922–31 include section: "The Woman voter," official organ of the National League of Women Voters.

"A preliminary investigation into the state of the native languages of South Africa, by C. M. Doke" (with bibliographical appendices): v. 7, p. [1]–98.

7:9. SUPPLEMENTS

Serial publications may be accompanied by supplements that are monographic or that are themselves serial publications. The former, if important, are described in the same manner as supplements to monographic publications. (See Chapter 5, Supplements, indexes, etc.) The latter may be described in a similar manner with a "dash" entry, but following the cataloging rules for serial publications. If they are likely to be known as independent works, or if they are to be classified separately, they are cataloged as independent entries.

Verein Deutscher Ingenieure, *Berlin.*
Zeitschrift. Bd. 1– 1857–
Berlin.

    v. illus., maps, diagrs. 30 cm.

—— —— Beihefte Verfahrenstechnik, Schriftenfolge für Chemie-Ingenieure, Apparatebauer und verwandte Berufe.
Folge 1937–
Berlin.

    v. illus., diagrs. 30 cm.

Blätter für Volksbibliotheken und Lesehallen. 1.–
Jahrg.; Jan./Feb. 1900–
Leipzig, O. Harrassowitz.

    v. 24 cm. bimonthly.

—— Ergänzungshefte. 1.–
Leipzig, O. Harrassowitz, 1905–

    no. diagrs. 24 cm.

    Ceased publication with no. 5 (1915) Cf. Union list of serials.

The Oregon state bar bulletin. v. 1–
Dec. 1935–
Portland.

    v. 26 cm. bimonthly (except Aug. and Oct.)

    Vols. 1– issued as a suppl. to the Oregon law review.

Irregular and unnumbered as well as unimportant supplements are noted informally.

> Unnumbered and undated supplements with title Bollettino accompany each number.
> Supplements accompany some numbers.
> Supplements accompany no. 6 and 10.

7:10. SPECIAL NUMBERS

Special numbers of serial publications present, as such, no particular problem of description. They are cataloged as separate works, with the relationship to the regular numbers shown, cataloged with analytical entries, or simply noted informaliy. If they are to be shelved with the regular numbers and are of minor importance, they may be disregarded.

a. As a separate work:

> Bertram, Anthony, 1897–
> Contemporary painting in Europe; introd. by Anthony Bertram. London, New York, The Studio ₁1939₁
>> 114 p. illus., col. plates. 30 cm.
>> "Special autumn number of the Studio, 1939."

> Shipping, commerce and aviation of Australia. 1935–
> Sydney, Shipping Newspapers.
>> v. illus. 38 cm. annual.
>> Special issues of the Daily commercial news and shipping list.

b. Noted informally:

> "Mélanges d'études anciennes offerts à Georges Radet": v. 42.

7:11. INDEXES

Indexes to single volumes of serial publications are not recorded. Other indexes are cataloged with the set which they index. They are recorded in a conventional, tabular form, or in an informal note, or by a combination of the two. The information given for each index includes some or all of the following items, and in this order:

a. Kind of index, i. e., author, subject, chronological, etc.

b. Volumes or numbers of the serial indexed.

c. Dates of the serial indexed.

d. Location of the index in the set, i. e., "in" if it is included in the paging of an issue, "with" if separately paged, or unpaged, and bound with a volume.

e. Statement of number of volumes of the index if not "in" or "with" a volume of the set.

f. Size of the index if it varies from the size of the set.

g. Other miscellaneous bibliographical data, such as the volume and number of the issue of the serial if the index comprises a whole number, or the number

to which the index is a supplement. Compilers of indexes are not ordinarily noted.

1. Tabular form.

INDEXES:

Vols. 1–9, 1881–90, *with* v. 9.
Vols. 10–15, 1891–96, *with* v. 15.
Vols. 1–20, 1881–1901, *with* v. 20.
Vols. 21–40, 1902–21, *in* v. 40.

INDEXES:

Author index.
Vols. 1–6, 1915–21, *with* v. 6.
Subject index.
Vols. 1–6, 1915–21, *with* v. 6.

INDEXES:

Subject index.
Vols. 1–11, July 1915–Dec. 1920. **1 v.**
Vols. 12–51, 1921–40 (Its Bulletin no. 696) **1 v.**

INDEXES:

No. 1–25, 1910–35 (Suppl. to no. 29) **1 v.**

INDEXES:

Vols. 1–22, 1918–Apr./June 1937. (Issued as **Publicación núm. 45 of** the Instituto Panamericano de Geografía e Historia) **2 v.**

INDEXES:

Vols. 1–7, 1874–Jan. 1884; ser. 2, v. 1–21, 1884–1904. **1 v.**
Ser. 2, v. 22–39, 1905–22. **1 v.**
Ser. 2, v. 40–44, 1922–27. **1 v.**

INDEXES:

1841–Nov. 1890. **1 v.** 19 cm.
1841–Feb. 1890. **1 v.** 19 cm.
Mar. 1899–Feb. 1905. **1 v.** 19 cm.
Mar. 1905–Feb. 1910. **1 v.** 19 cm.

INDEXES:

Indice sistemático.
Vols. 1–11, 1919–29, *in* v. 10, pt. 1.
Indice cronológico.
Vols. 1–11, 1919–29. (Issued as pt. 2 of v. 10 and 20) **1 v.**

INDEXES:

Vols. 1–100, 1832–56. **1 v.**
Vols. 101–116, 1857–60. **1 v.**
Vols. 117–164, 1861–72, and suppl. v. 1–8, *with* v. 101–116. **1 v.**

INDEXES:

Subject index.
Vols. 1–5, 1934–38 (Suppl. to v. 6, no. 1) *with* v. 5.
General index.
Vols. 1–10, 1934–43, *with* v. 10.

2. An informal note is used for a single index to a serial that has ceased publication and in other cases if the tabular form is impracticable.

> Includes index.
>
> Includes index, with special t. p. (London, Pitman, 1945)
>
> Index with v. 8.
>
> Index for v. 1–7, Mar. 1931–June 1935, with v. 7.
>
> Vol. 8], pt. 2, is index.
>
> Indexes cumulative from 1931 included annually in vols. for 1936–40; each vol., 1941–   includes an index covering the preceding ten-year period.

7:12. "BOUND WITHS"

If a second serial or a monograph is bound with a serial and cataloged separately, it is mentioned in the catalog entry for the serial in a "bound with" note. The form of this note varies from the form of note used in cataloging two monographs bound together, because of the necessity for showing exactly where the second publication is located, and, if the second publication is a serial, the issues of it that are included. For the same reasons the corresponding note in the entry for the monograph or the second serial varies from the form used in cataloging a work bound with a monographic publication.

The "bound with" notes consist of the name of the author of the serial (if any) in catalog entry form, brief title, size if it varies two or more centimeters from the size of the other work, and the specific issues contained in the work. If the serial cited in the note is entered under title, the dates covered by the volumes are also included in the note.

> The **Massachusetts** missionary magazine ... containing religious and interesting communications calculated to edify Christians and inform the rising generation ... v. 1–5; May 1803–May 1808. Boston, Printed by E. Lincoln.
>
> 5 v.   21 cm.   monthly.
>
> Bound with v. 2: Emmons, Nathanael. A sermon delivered before the Massachusetts Missionary Society, at their annual meeting in Boston, May 27, 1800. Charlestown, 1800.

> **Emmons, Nathanael,** 1785–1840.
>
> A sermon delivered before the Massachusetts Missionary Society, at their annual meeting in Boston, May 27, 1800. Charlestown, Printed and sold by S. Etheridge, 1800.
>
> 44 p.   21 cm.
>
> Bound with the Massachusetts missionary magazine, v. 2, May 1804–Apr. 1805.

> **Friends, Society of.** *American Friends Service Committee.*
>
> Spanish relief bulletin.   v. 1–
> May 26, 1937–
> Philadelphia, Committee on Spain, American Friends Service Committee.
>
> v. in   illus.   28 cm.   irregular.

Vols. 1–2, no. 1 bound with its Bulletin on relief in France, no. 1–54, its Bulletin on refugees abroad and at home, no. 1–18, and its Bulletin on relief in England, no. 1–17.

Friends, Society of. *American Friends Service Committee.*

Bulletin on relief in France. ₁no.₁ 1–
June 10, 1940–
Philadelphia.

no. in   v.   illus.   29 cm.   irregular.

No. 1–54 bound with its Spanish relief bulletin, v. 1–2, no. 1.

That same old coon. no. 1–25; Apr. 12–Nov. 16, 1844. **Dayton,** R. N. & W. F. Comly.

1 v.   46 cm.   weekly (irregular)

Bound with the Coon dissector, v. 1, no. 1–24, May 7–Nov. 22, 1844.

Coon dissector. v. 1, no. 1–24; May 7–Nov. 22, 1844. **Dayton,** A. H. Munn.

1 v.   illus.   46 cm.   weekly (irregular)

Bound with That same old coon, no. 1–25, Apr. 12–Nov. 16, 1844.

7:13. ANALYTICAL ENTRIES

Serials that are parts of other serials can generally be described by **means of an** informal note in the catalog entry for the main work. A cross reference **from the** title, or the author and title, of the part takes the place of an analytical **entry.**

Beginning with 1920, includes Oudheidkundige mededeelingen uit het Rijksmuseum van Oudheden.
Vols. 1–   include Proceedings of the 27th annual meeting of the Pacific Coast Branch of the American Historical Association.

Titles which are sufficiently important to require separate analytical **entries,** or for which special secondary entries need to be made, are cataloged **according** to the rules for cataloging other serial publications, with an analytical note taking the place of collation, or imprint and collation, as in other analytical entries. (See Chapter 6.) This note follows the form of other "in" analytical notes, the reference to the main work containing the same data as the "bound with" notes for serials. (See 7:12.)

American Historical Association.

Proceedings. ₁1st₁–   1884–
(*In its* Papers. 1884–88. New York. 25 cm.; *and in its* Annual report. 1889–91, 1893–1917, 1919–32, 1935–   Washington. 25 cm.)

8. Maps, Relief Models, Globes, and Atlases

8:1. MAPS

Certain distinctive characteristics of maps require special treatment in the catalog entry. Entry information for books is found, normally, on the title page. Similar information on maps is arranged to suit the space available on the sheet and the taste of the map designer. In applying to maps the descriptive cataloging rules for books, the whole face of a map is considered as its title page. Because maps are difficult to withdraw from, and return to, the files, descriptive notes in the catalog entry, which may aid in the selection or rejection of a particular map, are desirable. With these special qualifications, the rules for cataloging monographic publications and serials are applicable to maps except as specified in the following paragraphs.

A. *Title*. The title may be taken from any part of the face of the map. If two titles appear on the face of a map, the more applicable one is selected, with the variant title recorded in a note. Preference over a marginal title is given to a title within the border of the map, or within a cartouche, which, on early maps, often includes author, title, imprint, etc. If a base map has been overprinted, the overprinted title is used for the body of the entry. The dedication, in whole or in part, may be used as the title for early maps.

If the map lacks a title, one is supplied by the cataloger, preference being given to a title that has been used in reference sources to describe the same map. The title of another edition of the map may be used. If the title must be arbitrarily supplied, preference is given to the name of the area shown, in the form used on the map.

B. *Collation*. The collation consists of the number of maps with a statement of size. For a single map on one sheet, the word "map" or phrase "col. map" [1] is used. If printed on several sheets, but so designed that it would be incomplete without joining the parts, it is described as a single map; e. g., "map on 4 sheets." If, on the other hand, the work consists of a number of sheets, each of which has the characteristics of a complete map, it is described as a number of maps; e. g., "4 maps."

The height and width of the map are given in centimeters, any fraction being counted as a full centimeter. The measurement is taken from the outer edge of the border unless the map extends beyond the border; its greatest height or width is then measured. If it is difficult to measure the height and width of the map,

---

[1] Any map which would require more than one printing plate for reproduction (exclusive of colored military grid) is designated as a colored map. This includes hand-colored maps.

the sheet is measured.   For circular maps, the diameter, measured to include the border, is given.

> map 25 x 35 cm.
> col. map on sheet 45 x 33 cm.
> col. map 264 x 375 cm. on 9 sheets each 96 x 142 cm.
> 3 col. maps 78 x 113 cm.
> map 45 cm. in diameter.

If the size of the map is less than half the size of the sheet on which it is printed, both sizes are indicated.

> map 20 x 31 cm. on sheet 37 x 50 cm.

If a map is printed with an outer cover within which the map sheet is intended to be folded, or if the map sheet itself contains a panel or section designed to appear on the outside when the map is folded, the size of the map and the size of the sheet in folded form are both given.

> map 80 x 57 cm. fold. to 21 x 10 cm.
> col. map 9 x 20 cm. on sheet 40 x 60 cm. fold. to 21 x 10 cm.

Maps that are printed on both sides of a single sheet are described as follows:

> *Collation:* map 45 x 80 cm. on sheet 50 x 44 cm.
> *Note:* Printed on both sides of sheet, with line for joining indicated.

If the maps in a set, or sheets of a single map, vary in size, the size common to most of the maps is given with the appropriate qualification.

> 69 maps 45 x 55 cm. (1 map 60 x 90 cm.)
> 69 maps 45 x 55 cm. (some larger)
> 69 maps 45 x 55 cm. (some smaller)

If there is no size common to most of the maps, the greatest height of any of the maps and the greatest width of any of them are given, followed by the phrase "or smaller."

> 69 maps 60 x 90 cm. or smaller.

C. *Series note.*   Many maps are printed with series statements of two different publishing bodies.   In choosing the series for the normal series note position, preference is given to the one that is more closely related to the heading.   The second series is given in a note following the note that states the scale of the map.

D. *Scale.*   The scale of the map is given in the first paragraph after the collation, in the style indicated by examples below.   The word "Scale" is followed by the representative fraction, expressed as a ratio, if it is stated or can easily be ascertained.[2]   Additional scale information given on the map, such as a statement of comparative measures or limitation of the scale to particular parts of the map, is added.   Exact quotation with quotation marks is not necessary unless

---

[2] The representative fraction can be computed from a statement of scale in terms of equivalent measure on the map, or obtained from tables.   Commercial natural scale indicators are available by means of which a representative fraction can be approximated from a graphic scale expressed in miles, kilometers, or yards, or from the parallels of the map projection grid

(1) the statement presents unusual information that cannot be verified by the cataloger, (2) a direct quotation of the scale note is more precise than a scale note in conventional form, or (3) the statement on the map includes errors of grammar or spelling. If the scale is calculated from the graphic scale, the projection grid, or from other sources on the map, the fraction is qualified by the abbreviation "ca." If the representative fraction is computed arithmetically from a statement of approximate equivalence on the map, the qualification "ca." is also used.

> Scale 1:250,000 or 1 inch to 3.95 miles.
> Scale ca. 1:5,000,000.
> Scale 1:2,000,000.
> Scale 1:59,304,960.   Along meridians only, one inch=936 statute miles.

If the scale cannot be computed, or if a map is not drawn to scale, a note states this fact.

> Scale not given.
> Not drawn to scale.

If the scale is incorrectly given on the map, the correct representative fraction is stated, with the statement on the map following, in this form:

> Scale ca. 1:90,000 (not "1 inch to the mile")
> Scale ca. 1:90,000 (not "1:63,360")

If the entry describes maps drawn to two scales, both are given; e. g., Scale 1:100,000 and 1:200,000. If there are more than two, the note "Scales vary" is used.

E. *Other supplementary notes.* Except for the scale note, and a second series note (if any) which always follows it immediately, no definite order of notes can be prescribed. A logical sequence should be maintained as far as possible, but this need not be the same for every map. The following are the types of information frequently mentioned in supplementary notes and the approximate order of these notes in the catalog entry.

1. *Composite sets of maps.* A working collection of any set of maps consists of the latest issue of each sheet. The various sheets of a set may be revised as need arises. Such revision may be the result of a change in the cultural or natural features of the area, increased knowledge of the area, or replenishment of the stock of the sheets which makes possible the incorporation of minor changes which would not otherwise justify revision. Thus a complete second, third, etc., edition of a set may never result. A composite set consists of sheets of various editions and issues. Though a complete working set of maps may be in the collection, the entry is not closed until it is known that publication has ceased. This practice requires a note stating, if possible, what constitutes a complete set. A statement of the fact that the various editions and issues are cataloged as a single set is given if variant issues of any sheets are known. The position of this note is maintained even if other types of information are combined with it.

> Complete in 174 sheets. Set includes various issues of some sheets, including some reissued by U. S. Army Map Service. Some sheets, prepared under the direction of the Chief of Engineers, U. S. Army, have series designation: Provisional G. S. G. S. 4145.

2. *Source of title.*

> Title from verso.
> Title from cover.
> "₍The title₎ is taken from the copy in the Public Record Office ₍London₎ upon which it is found in the form of an engrossed inscription."—Notes on the Southack map. Boston, 1717.

3. *Defects of imperfect copy being cataloged.*

4. *Information supplementary to the body of the entry.*

> In upper margin:
> Also entitled:
> Title on outside, when folded:

5. *Physical description.* The physical characteristics of a map may limit its usefulness or enhance its value. Its physical description may aid in its identification; for example, the watermark of the paper may be a mark of identification for maps of the eighteenth century and earlier.

> Blue line print.
> Produced photographically.
> Photocopy (positive) from the copy in the Yale University Library.
> Photocopy (positive) from manuscript original in the William L. Clements Library.
> In envelope, with title on flap.
> Watermark: C & I Honig.

6. *Limit of issue.* Official maps often bear a note of security classification, as "Secret," "Confidential," "Restricted," "For use of Army and Navy Department agencies only. Not for sale or distribution," "For official use only," etc. Since security classification is subject to change, it is not considered to be a critical item of identification and is not given in the catalog entry.

7. *Special cartographic information.* The name of the map projection is given if stated or if sufficiently unusual to affect the use of the map. The prime meridian is named if other than that of Greenwich.

> "Polyconic projection."
> Prime meridians: Ferro and Paris.
> Military grid.
> Oriented with north to the right.
> "Meridians are based on the meridian of Rome, which is 12°27'7.1" east of Greenwich."
> Prime meridians: Washington and Greenwich.

8. *Nature and scope of work.* Notes are given to clarify an indefinite or misleading title and to aid in the selection or rejection of the map. Matter of unusual interest to map users is noted. Acquaintance with maps will enable the map cataloger to recognize certain features as common to most maps of certain classes.

It is the uncommon item, the extra, unexpected information that a map gives which must be noted. For example, although roads are commonly shown on medium or large scale maps, it is unusual for the roads to be classified as to surface, width, etc.; a note of this fact is made in cataloging a map giving this information.

> Shows most of Canada and all of Mexico and Central America.
> > (*Map has title: United States.*)
>
> Title and place names in Arabic script.
>
> Place names in Italian.
> > (*Title and dedication in Latin.*)
>
> "Contours at 10 meter intervals."
>
> Shows 4 classes of railroads, 5 classes of roads and tracks, and 3 types of internal boundaries.
>
> Except for title and "La mer du Nord" the map is in English.

9. *Notes on authorship, including editors, engravers, etc.* The work of every person named as having had a hand in or direct responsibility for an early map is recorded in supplementary notes if it is not shown by the body of the entry.

10. *Notes showing relationship to other works.*

> With this is issued:
> Red overprinting on the author's Greater Germany: administrative divisions 1 July 1944 (No. 3817–R & A, OSS)

11. *Bibliographical history of the work.* Notes are made in regard to variant editions or issues. When cataloging early engraved maps, several copies may be at hand. Some effort is made to determine whether they are identical, or whether changes have been made in content without change of title or imprint. Variant issues are normally listed by a "dash entry" as another issue, with a brief note indicating differences. (See 4:1, Issues.) If the issues of such a map are undated, but can, from internal evidence, be dated with some degree of accuracy, each may be cataloged separately.

If a detailed study of a map is known to have been published, the copy in hand is identified with reference to the published study, and a note of such identification made.

Most maps are compiled from various sources, which may or may not be listed. If it is known that a map has been based on a single source map, the source is noted.

> Copied from
> Based on
> Probably a revision of the 1st ed. of Maury's Washington map of the United States. A later ed., with many changes, lacks date.
> "A facsimile of the original 'map in the John Carter Brown Library, Providence, Rhode Island, 1942. Reproduced in collotype by the Meriden Gravure Company."
> Differs from an earlier ed. by the copyright notice in the upper left margin, replacing name of engraver, and by the inclusion of "United States territory" between "Tennassee [sic]" and "Georgia."

12. *Contents.* A partial contents note is made to bring out important parts of a map, especially marginal or inset maps. If a collective title is given for a num-

ber of insets, that title is used, followed, in parentheses, by the number of items. Numerous small or unimportant insets may be covered by a general note. If insets to be listed surround the map, the listing ordinarily begins in the upper left corner and proceeds in clockwise sequence.

> Key to 140 place names included.
> Includes "Glossary."
> Marginal diagram: ₁Index to₁ adjoining sheets.
> Insets: ₁Alaska₁—Hawaiian Islands.
> Includes 5 insets.
> Numerous insets of various landing fields included on each sheet.
> Insets, on reduced ₁or enlarged₁ scale:

Items on the verso of the map are noted in a new paragraph following the list of insets. The note begins with the phrase "On verso."

> On verso: New map of South Hadley, Mass. ₁Scale ca. 1:15,000₁

13. *Peculiarities of the copy being described.*

F. *Two or more maps on one sheet.* If several maps are printed on a single sheet, one of four ways of cataloging them is followed.

1. If there is a collective title, it is used in the body of the entry and the titles of the individual maps are shown in a contents note if individual listing is desirable.

2. If there are several maps on one side of a sheet and no collective title, the several titles may be included in the body of the entry or one title may be given there and the others in a note.

3. Of two maps on opposite sides of a sheet, without a collective title, one may be chosen for cataloging as the principal map with the other mentioned in a note.

4. If a second map is important enough, an analytical entry is made for it. (See G below.)

G. *Analytical entries.* An analytical entry may be made for a map which is included in a book, or which is an inset on another map, or which is printed on the same sheet with another map. The entry is prepared according to the rules for other analytical entries (see Chapter 6), the "analytical note" being introduced by the appropriate word or phrase: "In," "Inset on" or "On verso of."

Detached maps follow rules prescribed for detached parts of books. (See 4:3.)

8:2. RELIEF MODELS

The term "relief model"[3] is used to denote a three-dimensional map other than a globe. Characteristic differences from other maps are shown in the collation statement, in the statement of scale, and in the physical description.

A. *Collation.* The collation of a relief model follows the rules for maps except that the word "map" is replaced by the term "relief model."

---

[3] The term "relief map" has been used so often for two-dimensional maps designed to portray relief, that the term is avoided in exact description.

B. *Scale*. The horizontal scale is given in the same form as for a map, followed by the vertical scale expressed as a ratio or exaggeration of the horizontal scale.

> Scale 1:1,000,0᾽0; vertical scale 6 times the horizontal.

C. *Note of physical description*. The material of which the model is constructed (plaster, papier-mâché, rubber, plastic, etc.) is stated.

8:3. GLOBES

A globe is a map drawn, mounted, or constructed on a sphere to give a more true representation of the earth, or to represent the relative positions of certain heavenly bodies as viewed from the earth. Except for the collation statement, the cataloging of globes follows the rules prescribed for the cataloging of maps.

For terrestrial globes, the word "globe" takes the place of "map," and the diameter is given. A celestial globe is designated "celestial globe."

8:4. ATLASES

The cataloging of atlases varies from general book cataloging practice in only two respects, as follows:

A. *Collation*. To distinguish an atlas from a set of loose maps and to aid in identifying copies and distinguishing between editions, the collation given represents the pages or leaves of text and the number of maps, or the pages or leaves of maps (or a combination of these) according to the make-up of the atlas. If a separate section of numbered maps is also paged the number of maps is ignored.

> [1] l., 148 col. maps. 26 x 40 cm.
> xiii p., 30 l. of col. maps. 40 cm.
> 198 p. of maps. 32 cm.
> 19 p., 152 p. of maps (part col.), [21] p. 27 cm.

Maps not forming a separate section are described in the same manner as maps in works that are not atlases.

> 48 p. maps. 31 x 42 cm.
> xi, iv, 266, 149 p. illus., maps (126 col.) 43 cm.
> 416 (i. e. 428) p. col. illus., 145 maps (part col.) 36 cm.

B. *Scale*. If all the maps, except index maps, are of one or two scales, a supplementary note states the scale. This note is placed with notes on physical description. (See 8:1 D.)

> Scale of maps 1:2,500,000 or 1:5,000,000.
> Scale of maps 1:4,800 or 1 inch to 400 feet, and 1:3,600 or 1 inch to 300 feet.

C. *Note of physical geography.* The reverse of which [?]... (physical) projection, relief, physiographic [?] ...

8.3. GLOBES

A globe is a map drawn, mounted, or constructed on a sphere to give a more true representation of the earth, or to represent the whole... position of certain heavenly bodies as viewed from the earth's center. Except for the globe not sustaining the cataloging of globes [...] the rules prescribed for the cataloging of maps... For terrestrial globes, the word "globe" takes the place of "area," and the diameter is given. A celestial globe is described [...]

8.4. ATLASES

The catalogue of atlases varies from a general book cataloging practice in [...] two respects, as follows:

A. Atlases [...] bibliographic, or atlas bound set of loose maps and [...] in determining scope and distinguishing between editions, the collation gives [...] sents the pages or leaves of text and the number of maps [...] of maps are a combination of these according to [...]

[...several faded lines, largely illegible...]

B. *Scale.* If all the maps, except index maps, are of the same [...] supplementary note states the scale. This is not placed with notes [...] description. (See § 4.1 D.)

9. Music

9:1. INTRODUCTION

The principles of descriptive cataloging apply to music as well as to other kinds of materials, the description of music following the general rules as far as they are applicable. Because of the way in which music is published, however, certain exceptions and additions to the general rules must be made. Only the exceptions and additions, i. e., the treatment of the special types of information of particular importance to the musician, are given in this section.

The following types of information are included in the catalog entry whenever they are applicable to the work in hand and ascertainable by the cataloger with a reasonable expenditure of time.

a. Medium of performance, including alternative and optional instruments.

b. Indication of whether or not the work consists of score and/or musical parts for performance.

c. Statement that the work is an arrangement or other special version, with indication of the original form.

d. Name of the arranger.

e. Type of notation, if of a special nature.

f. Duration of performance.

9:2. CONVENTIONAL TITLES

Conventional titles are filing titles established according to rule and included in the catalog entry [1] in order (a) to identify and bring together in the catalog all editions and arrangements of a composition and (b) to bring together in a systematic arrangement general and miscellaneous collections of a composer's works. The precedent for this treatment comes from similar usages in the cataloging of the works of voluminous authors such as Goethe and Shakespeare and in the cataloging of editions of the Bible. The necessity for this device is particularly great in the field of music because of the widespread use by composers of all periods of titles consisting of names of musical forms and because of the fact that musical compositions are frequently issued in numerous editions with variations in the language and the wording of the title pages. Editions of Beethoven's opus 27, no. 2 are cited below with their titles, as an example of such variations.

> Beethoven's Moonlight sonata. Op. 27, no. 2.
> Deux sonates (quasi fantaisies) No. 2, Ut min.

---

[1] In Library of Congress entries, the conventional title is enclosed in brackets and printed in eight-point type at title indention beneath the heading. Between the conventional title and the transcription of the title appearing on the work a space is left for another conventional title for those libraries that do not wish to use the one chosen by the Library of Congress.

Gran sonata per cembalo o pianoforte, opera 27, n. 2.
Klaviersonate in Cis moll, Op. 27, No. 2.
Sonata, Do min. (Chiaro di luna) Op. 27, n. 2.
Sonata (Moonlight) in C sharp minor. Op. 27, no. 2.
Sonata quasi una fantasia per il clavicembalo o pianoforte. Opera 27. No. 2.
    (*Original title.*)
Sonate, Op. 27, Nr. 2 (Die sogenannte Mondscheinsonate)
Zwei Sonaten in Form von Fantasien. Op. 27, No. 2.

Composer-title cross references are made from forms of the title not used as the conventional title, as may be advisable; e. g.,

Beethoven, Ludwig van, 1770–1827. Moonlight sonata
    see his Sonata, piano, no. 14, op. 27, no. 2, C# minor.

In the selection and construction of conventional titles the best bibliographical sources are consulted. These include thematic indexes, bibliographies, complete editions of composers' works, standard biographies and music encyclopedias. Information given in the work cataloged is not used in the conventional title without an attempt at verification. However, if verification is impossible, such information may be used unless there is reason to doubt its accuracy.

Although most music which is entered under a composer heading is assigned a conventional title, it may not always be necessary or advisable to establish it at the time of cataloging. If this decision is made, the line normally occupied by the conventional title is left blank. Situations in which a conventional title may not be established are, first, if the title page title is the same as the conventional title would be, at least as far as the filing of the card is concerned, and it seems unlikely that there will be any need for a conventional title in the future, and second, if it is impossible to obtain the information required for a conventional title.

A. *Selection.* The title preferred for the conventional title, with the qualification appearing in the following paragraph, is (or is based on) that of the first edition.[2]

Auber, Daniel François Esprit, 1782–1871.
    ₍Le dieu et la bayadère ...₎ [3]
    La bayadère amoureuse, Le dieu et la bayadère.

The selection of the conventional title may in some cases be influenced by the titles of other works by the composer, as when a work which is part of a numbered series of works bearing the same general title has a particular title of its own.

---

[2] The works of Russian composers first published in Russia often have title pages in several languages, of which the first is commonly French; the covers are generally entirely in Russian. In such cases the Russian title is considered the original unless evidence shows that the composer's own title was in some other language.

[3] Various elements necessary to complete the conventional title have been omitted from some of the examples used in the early paragraphs of this section in order to avoid irrelevant considerations.

Beethoven, Ludwig van, 1770–1827.
₁Symphony, no. 3 ...₁
Sinfonia eroica.

B. *Modifications of the title selected.* Laudatory adjectives in the title, which are frequently encountered in publications around 1800, such as "grand," "celebrated," "favorite," etc., are omitted unless they are an integral part of the title. Cardinal numbers are omitted unless they form an integral part of the title.

₁Sonatas ...₁
12 sonatas.

₁Trios ...₁
Three trios.

₁The Ten commandments₁
The Ten commandments.

Ordinal numbers, and words indicating medium of performance when used in conjunction with the names of types of musical compositions, are treated as supplementary elements following the title.

₁Sonata, piano, no. 1 ...₁
First sonata for the piano.

₁Quartet, strings ...₁
String quartet.

C. *Language.* The choice of language for the conventional title depends upon which of the following paragraphs is applicable.

1. *Titles consisting solely of certain names of types of compositions.* For a title which consists solely of the name of a type of composition, if there are cognate forms of the name in English, Italian, French and German (or if the same term is used in all of these languages), the accepted English form is generally employed. In case of doubt, a standard music dictionary is consulted. Exception is made for études, the original language being preferred. In the case of a prelude and fugue, the English phrase is also used.

Beethoven, Ludwig van, 1770–1827.
₁Symphony, no. 5 ...₁
Fünfte Symphonie.

Geminiani, Francesco, 1687–1762.
₁Sonatas ...₁
Sonate a violino, violone e cembalo.

Geminiani, Francesco, 1687–1762.
₁Concerti grossi ...₁
Six concerti grossi for 2 violins, viola and violoncello soli with strings and harpsichord.

Wieck, Friedrich, 1785–1873.
₁Studien, piano ...₁
Piano studies.

77

2. *Other titles.* If the original title is in one of the languages most commonly read in this country (English, French, German, Italian, Spanish, Portuguese and Latin) it is retained as the conventional title.

> **Gaubert, Philippe,** 1879–
> ₍Le chevalier et la damoiselle₎
> Le chevalier et la damoiselle, ballet en 2 actes de Serge Lifar d'après une légende médiévale; musique de Philippe Gaubert.

> **Strauss, Johann,** 1825–1899.
> ₍Der Zigeunerbaron ...₎
> The gypsy baron, romantic opera in 3 acts and a prologue.

If the title is in a language other than one of those above, the title in most common use in the United States is used as the conventional title.[4] Other factors being equal, English is preferred.

> **Dohnányi, Ernö,** 1877–
> ₍Essential finger exercises₎
> A legfontosabb ujjgyakorlatok.

> **Rimskiĭ-Korsakov, Nikolai Andreevich,** 1844–1908.
> ₍Le coq d'or ...₎
> The golden cockerel.

If no title in one of the above-named languages is found to be in common use in this country, one of the following procedures is employed:

a. The title in the original language is used. If this language is one with a non-Roman alphabet, it is transliterated.

> **Chernomordikov, David Aronovich.**
> ₍Vpered₎
> Гимн рабочему народу "Вперег."
>   *Title transliterated:* Gimn rabochemu narodu "Vpered."

b. A provisional conventional title in one of the above-named languages is used.

c. The use of a conventional title is deferred.

D. *Medium of performance.* The conventional title generally includes a statement of the medium of performance only if the title proper consists of (or, in instrumental music, contains) the name of a type of musical composition. This is followed, after a comma, with a concise statement of the instrumental and/or vocal medium for which it was intended.

> ₍Sonata, piano₎
> ₍Morceaux faciles, piano₎
> ₍Sahara suite, 2 pianos₎
> ₍Variations on a rococo theme, violoncello & orchestra₎
> ₍Trios, women's voices & piano₎

---

[4] Factors determining such usage are the form of title used in editions available in the United States, in programs of concerts and opera houses in this country and in English language music dictionaries and encyclopedias.

In the following cases the medium is not stated:

If the medium is implied by the title; e. g.,

Chorale-prelude (implied medium: organ)

Mass (implied medium: voices, with or without accompaniment)

Songs or lieder (implied medium: solo voice, with accompaniment for keyboard stringed instrument)

Symphony (implied medium: orchestra)

(If, however, the medium is other than that implied by the title, it is stated; e. g., ₁Symphony, organ₁)

If the work consists of a collection of compositions with the same title but for different media.

Defesch, Willem, *d. ca.* 1760.
 ₁Sonatas₁
 12 sonatas, six for a violin, with a thorough bass, several of them are proper for a German flute, and six for two violoncellos.

If the medium is not specifically designated by the composer.

McLamb, Margaret Dudley, 1929–
 ₁Suite₁
 Suite for three melody instruments.

The statement of medium is as specific as a maximum limitation of three component elements will allow. Score order is followed with these exceptions: (a) in works for a keyboard instrument (not including figured bass) and more than one other instrument, the keyboard instrument is named first, (b) voices are always named first. If there is more than one part for a given type of instrument or voice the appropriate arabic numeral is prefixed to its designation in the statement of medium unless the title makes this unnecessary.

₁Sonata, violin & piano₁
₁Trio, piano, clarinet & violoncello₁
₁Canons, women's voices & piano₁
₁Scherzo, 2 flutes & 2 clarinets₁
₁Quartet, flutes & clarinets₁

1. *Full instrumental ensembles.* For instrumental combinations intended for more performers than there are musical parts, such terms as "orchestra," (used for full orchestra, chamber orchestra, small orchestra, etc.) "string orchestra," and "band" are used.

Berkeley, Lennox, 1903–
 ₁Nocturne, orchestra₁
 Nocturne for orchestra.

The statement of medium for concertos, concertinos and concertantes for solo instrument(s) and orchestra consists only of the name of the solo instrument(s), unless the accompaniment is other than orchestra, in which case it is also named.

If the word "concerto" is modified by a distinctive adjective or phrase, a full statement of medium is made.

> ₁Concerto, violin₁
> ₁Concerto, violin & violoncello₁
> ₁Concerto, violin & string orchestra₁
> ₁Alameia concerto, piano & orchestra₁

For works called concerto, concertino or concertante but which were written without accompaniment, the abbreviation "unacc." is added to the name of the instrument.

> ₁Concerto, organ unacc.₁

In the case of concerti grossi the medium of performance is not specified, but the catalog entry shows (either in the body of the entry or in a supplementary note) the instruments of the solo group.

2. *Chamber music and solo instrumental music*. In instrumental music where there is to be but one performer to a part, the medium is expressed in one of, or in a combination of, the following ways given in order of preference: (a) by one of the names of certain standard chamber music combinations, (b) by designation of individual instruments, or (c) by designation of groups of instruments.

a. *Standard combinations*. For the following standard chamber music combinations specific designation of instruments is regarded as superfluous, a more concise statement being preferred:

Combination	Instrumental components
string trio	violin, viola & violoncello
string quartet	2 violins, viola & violoncello
piano trio	piano, violin & violoncello
piano quartet	piano, violin, viola & violoncello
piano quintet	piano, 2 violins, viola & violoncello

If the conventional title of a work for one of the above combinations begins with or contains "Trio," "Quartet," or "Quintet," the statement of medium will be either "strings" or "piano & strings."

> ₁Trio, piano & strings₁
> ₁Fantasy quintet, strings₁

If the title of a work for one of these combinations does not show that the work is a "Trio," "Quartet," or "Quintet," the statement of medium will be the name of the appropriate standard combination.

> ₁Serenade, piano quartet₁

All trios, quartets, and quintets for strings, or for piano and strings, which are for combinations of instruments other than those listed above are, however, to have a full statement of medium, even if more than three instruments must be named.

> ₁Quartet, violin, violas & violoncello₁
> ₁Quartet, violin, viola, violoncello & double bass₁

b. *Individual instruments.* English terminology is used as far as possible. The preferred terms in certain special cases are listed below.

> double bass (*not* bass viol)
> English horn
> horn (*not* French horn)
> recorder
> viola da gamba (*not* gamba)
> violoncello (*not* cello)

The term "piano" is used for one instrument, two hands; "2 pianos" is used for two instruments, four hands. If the number of hands varies from these, the information is included in the statement of medium: e. g., "piano, 4 hands," "2 pianos, 8 hands," etc.

The key in which instruments are pitched is omitted and alternative instruments are not named. The terms "alto," "tenor," "bass," etc., when preceding the names of instruments, are omitted if more than one such term would be required in the statement of medium.

In ensemble music composed before the end of the eighteenth century, the accompaniment for keyboard or other chordal instrument is customarily represented by a figured bass part only, the performer being expected to develop, or "realize," a complete accompaniment from this bass, *ex tempore*. Such a part, whether designated as basso continuo, general bass, figured bass, thorough bass, or continuo, is named in the conventional title merely as "continuo."

> Marcello, Benedetto, 1686–1729.
>   ₗSonatas, flute & continuoₗ
>   XII suonate a flauto solo, con il suo basso continuo per
> violoncello o cembalo.

However, if one of the parts of a work for orchestra or string orchestra is a figured bass, it is treated as part of the ensemble.

> Vivaldi, Antonio, 1690 (*ca.*)–1741.
>   ₗConcertos, flute & string orchestraₗ
>   6 Concerti für Flöte, Streichorchester und Generalbass
> (Cembalo oder Klavier)

Music for keyboard instruments composed before 1800 may have been intended by the composer for a particular instrument, for any keyboard stringed instrument (harpsichord, clavichord or piano),[5] or for organ. If a particular instrument is not designated, the following rules are applied:

If the work seems to have been intended for performance on any of the keyboard stringed instruments, of the player's choice or at his convenience, the term "harpsichord" is used if the work was composed prior to 1760, the word "piano" if it was composed in or after 1760.[6] If the period of composition cannot be de-

---

[5] "Cembalo" is translated "Harpsichord."
[6] "Harpsichord" is used for modern music intended for that instrument.

termined, the date of the first publication determines the term to be used. If the application of this rule results in the separation of a given composer's works between harpsichord or clavichord and piano, the instrument for which the major portion of the works in a given category was intended is chosen for all of the works in that category.

If the work seems to have been intended for performance on any of the keyboard instruments including organ, the phrase "keyboard instrument" is used.

> **Albrechtsberger, Johann Georg,** 1736–1790.
>> ₍Fugues, keyboard instrument₎
>> Douze fugues pour le clavecin ou l'orgue.

c. *Groups of instruments.* If required, the following terms for groups of instruments are used: wood-winds, brasses, winds (for wood-winds plus brasses), percussion, plectral instruments, keyboard instruments, and strings.

>> ₍Quartet, strings₎
>> ₍Divertimento, piano & wood-winds₎
>> ₍Fanfare, brasses & percussion₎

3. *Vocal music.* The most common group designations for voices are: mixed voices, men's voices, women's voices, unison voices, and solo voices; the most common designations for solo voices are: soprano, mezzo-soprano, alto, tenor, baritone, and bass.

It often happens, particularly with music of the Renaissance period, that the most common and most convenient way of distinguishing groups of choral works is by the total number of voice parts. If the original titles or reliable bibliographies justify this method, it is used in the statement of medium in the conventional title.

>> ₍Madrigals, 5 part₎
>> ₍Madrigals, 8 part₎

Songs, part-songs and choruses without accompaniment are so indicated unless they are of a type which would normally be unaccompanied.

>> ₍Choruses, mixed voices, unacc.₎
>> ₍Trios, women's voices, unacc.₎
>> ₍Motets, mixed voices₎

If songs, chansons, lieder, etc., have an accompaniment for other than a keyboard stringed instrument alone, the medium of the accompaniment is followed by the abbreviation "acc."

>> ₍Chansons, guitar acc.₎

E. *Identifying elements.* No two works by the same composer are to have the same conventional title. Since titles which consist solely of the name of a type of composition typically require supplementary identifying data, such data are given in the conventional titles for all such works, to prevent future conflict.

Other titles, however, conflict but rarely. When they do, either a statement of medium, or a descriptive term within parentheses, is used for each of the works which must be distinguished. If, after using one of these devices, there is still a

conflict, one of the identifying elements described in paragraphs 1 to 4 below is
used to distinguish the works.

Medium statement:

> ₁Images, orchestra₁
> ₁Images, piano₁

Descriptive term:

> ₁Goyescas (Opera)₁
> ₁Goyescas (Piano work)₁
> ₁Tu es Petrus (Motet) no. 1₁
> ₁Tu es Petrus (Motet) no. 2₁
> ₁Tu es Petrus (Offertory)₁

If the title consists solely of the name of a type of composition, all, or as many
as can be readily ascertained, of three common identifying elements are included
in the conventional title in the following order: (1) serial number, (2) opus or
thematic index number and (3) key. These elements are separated by commas.

1. *Serial number.* If works with the same title and for the same medium are
consecutively numbered this information is included.

> ₁Quartet, strings, no. 2 ... ₁

2. *Opus or thematic index number.* Opus number, if any, and if easily ascertainable, is included.

If the work cataloged is one number from an opus consisting of several numbers,
the number of the work cataloged is added to the opus number, following a comma.

> ₁Preludes, piano, op. 17, no. 3₁

In the case of certain important composers, numbers assigned to the works in
recognized thematic indexes are used in the absence of, or in preference to, opus
numbers. These numbers are preceded by the initial letter of the bibliographer's
name; e. g., K. 453 (from Ludwig Köchel's *Chronologisch-thematisches Verzeichniss
sämtlicher Tonwerke Wolfgang Amade Mozarts.* 3. Aufl.).

If there is an unresolved conflict in opus numbering among works of the same
title and medium or if the overall opus numbering of a composer's works is confused and conflicting, the opus number is qualified by adding, within parentheses,
the name of the publisher originally using the number chosen.

> **Cambini, Giovanni Giuseppe,** 1746–1825.
> ₁Duets, flute & violin, op. 20 (Bland)₁
> Six favorite duets for a German flute and violin. Op. 20.
> London, J. Bland ₁179–?₁
>
> **Cambini, Giovanni Giuseppe,** 1746–1825.
> ₁Duets, flute & violin, op. 20 (Le Duc)₁
> Six duos pour flutte et violon. Œuvre 20. Paris, Le Duc
> ₁177–₁

3. *Key.* The key is ordinarily included in conventional titles of works composed in the period 1700–1900 and having titles consisting solely of (or, for instru-

mental works, containing) the name of a type of composition. If the mode is other than major or minor or if it is uncertain, it is not stated. For twentieth century works with such titles, the key is included only if designated or if there would otherwise be a conflict and the key can be readily ascertained.

> **Mendelssohn-Bartholdy, Felix,** 1809–1847.
>> ₍Trio, piano & strings, op. 66, C minor₎
>> ... Trio. Op. 66. Piano, violin & violoncello.
>
> **Reizenstein, Franz.**
>> ₍Sonata, piano, B₎
>> Sonata in B for pianoforte.
>
> **Babin, Victor,** 1908–
>> ₍Sonata-fantasia, violoncello & piano₎
>> Sonata-fantasia, for violoncello & piano.

4. *Other identifying elements.* If two works cannot be distinguished by the identifying elements described above, either because they are not available or because they are insufficient, the date of first publication is added, within parentheses, after other identifying elements, if any. If the date of publication is known to differ from the date of composition, a note is added reading "First published in ... " In the case of unpublished music the date of composition is used in the conventional title. In default of date, any identifying term such as place of composition or name of first publisher may be used, within parentheses.

F. *Two works published together.* When two works are published together, the conventional title used is that of the first work. A composer-title added entry (with title in conventional form but without brackets) is made for the second work. However, if the two works form a consecutively numbered group within a numbered series, they are treated as a collection. (See G 2, below.)

> **Chopin, Fryderyk Franciszek,** 1810–1849.
>> ₍Ballades₎
>> Balladen und Impromptus. Universal-Ed.
>> I. Chopin, Fryderyk Franciszek, 1810–1849. Impromptus.

G. *Collections.* If a composer first issues several of his works as a set or collection containing three or more works, this set or collection is assigned a conventional title as hitherto described.

>> ₍Ariettes oubliées₎
>> ₍Fantasiestücke, piano, op. 12₎
>> ₍Trio-sonatas, violins & continuo, op. 4₎

If an editor, compiler or publisher reissues several or all of a composer's works in the form of a collection, a conventional title is constructed without reference to the title of the collection in order to bring together works in the same form and/or medium and to provide a logical and useful filing place for such collections.

1. *Complete collections.* Editions of the complete works of a composer have as conventional title the word "Works."

a. *Works in one broad medium.* Collections containing various types of chamber, instrumental, or vocal music have as conventional title one of the following:

ʰWorks, chamber musicʰ
ʰWorks, instrumentalʰ
ʰWorks, vocalʰ

b. *Works in one specific medium.* Collections containing various types of works for one specific medium have as conventional title the word "Works" followed by a statement of the medium.

ʰWorks, chorusʰ
ʰWorks, orchestraʰ
ʰWorks, pianoʰ
ʰWorks, violinʰ

c. *Works in one form.* Collections consisting of works in one musical form or category have as their conventional title the name of such form or category followed by a statement of the medium unless the medium is obvious or unless several media are represented, in which cases no such statement is made.

ʰConcertosʰ
ʰConcertos, pianoʰ
ʰSonatasʰ
ʰSongsʰ ⁶

2. *Incomplete collections.* In all the above cases the conventional titles that are specified indicate completeness, or at least substantial and intended completeness, within the stated limits. If a collection is not complete within the stated limits, the word "Selections" is added, after a period. If, however, the selections form a consecutively numbered group within a numbered series, the inclusive numbers are added following a comma.

ʰWorks. Selectionsʰ
ʰWorks, organ. Selectionsʰ
ʰSonatas, violin & continuo, op. 3. Selectionsʰ
ʰSonatas, violin & continuo, op. 3, no. 7–12ʰ
ʰSymphonies, no. 1–3ʰ

H. *Excerpts.*⁷ The conventional title of an excerpt consists of the conventional title of the complete work from which it is drawn followed by a period and the title of the excerpt.

ʰRienzi. Overtureʰ
ʰAida. Celeste Aidaʰ

---

⁶ The term "Songs" is used only for collections originally bearing this title and for collections of works in this form which originally had miscellaneous titles. In the conventional title for collections first published by the composer as "Gesänge," "Lieder," "Romances," etc., the original title is used.

⁷ Excerpts are considered to exclude single numbers of a group of works with the same title published as a set or opus (e. g., one étude from a set of études). Treatment for such works is described in the preceding paragraph.

If the work is a movement from a work in more than one movement, the tempo designation may be used as excerpt title.

₁Symphony, no. 1, op. 21, C major.   Andante cantabile con moto₁

If all the components of a collective work have both title and number, the numbers are ignored.   If all the components have numbers but only some have titles, the number of the excerpt is used, following the title of the collective work and a period, and is itself followed by a comma and the title of the excerpt if there is such title.

> ₁Kinderscenen. Träumerei₁
> ₁Album für die Jugend. No. 30₁
> ₁Album für die Jugend. No. 10, Fröhliche Landmann₁

I. *Cadenzas.* The conventional title for a separately published cadenza consists of the word "Cadenza" following the conventional title of the concerto for which it was written. If the cadenza was written by a person other than the composer, this person's name, within parentheses, is added after the word "Cadenza."

> **Mozart, Johann Chrysostom Wolfgang Amadeus, 1756–1791.**
> ₁Concerto, flute, K. 285ᵈ (314) D major. Cadenzas (Barrère)₁
> Cadenzas for the flute concerto in D major (K. 314) ₁of₁ Mozart.

J. *Arrangements.* If a work has undergone any considerable simplification, amplication or alteration, this fact is shown in the conventional title by adding, following a semicolon, the abbreviation for "arranged." [8]

> **Beethoven, Ludwig van, 1770–1827.**
> ₁Works, piano. Selections; arr.₁
> Beethoven for ten little fingers.

> **Händel, Georg Friedrich, 1685–1759.**
> ₁The Messiah. Hallelujah; arr.₁
> The Hallelujah chorus arranged for band.

If the arrangement is made by the composer himself, it is treated as an original work, unless it bears the same identifying element or elements, such as opus or serial number, as the work arranged.

> **Ravel, Maurice, 1875–1937.**
> ₁Pavane pour une infante défunte, orchestra₁
> ₁Pavane pour une infante défunte, piano₁

> **Brahms, Johannes, 1833–1897.**
> ₁Symphony, no. 3, op. 90, F major; arr.₁

K. *Adaptations..* If the text, plot, setting or other literary or dramatic element, and the title of a musico-dramatic work are altered to suit the requirements of a new performance, with the music remaining essentially the same, the

---

[8] A realized continuo is not considered to be an arrangement.

conventional title of the work consists of the conventional title of the original work, followed, within parentheses, by the title of the adaptation.

> **Strauss, Johann,** 1825–1899.
>
> ₁Die Fledermaus₁
> ₁Die Fledermaus (Champagne sec)₁
> ₁Die Fledermaus (Gay Rosalinda)₁
> ₁Die Fledermaus (Rosalinda)₁

If new text is added to an earlier vocal or instrumental work and the title altered, this rule for adaptations is applied.

L. *Types of music requiring special treatment.* Because of peculiar difficulties encountered in the cataloging of certain types of music, as in the cases below, special treatment, either additional or contrary to those outlined heretofore, is required in order to assure satisfactory conventional titles.

1. *Works in the larger vocal forms.* For works in the larger vocal forms, such as operas, operettas, oratorios, cantatas and masses, the following subdivisions are used in the conventional title, following the title proper and a period:

a. "Libretto," for editions of the text alone. [9]

b. "Piano ₁or "Organ"₁-vocal score," for all editions in which the vocal accompaniment is either for piano or organ, original or arranged. In case of doubt as to which of these terms should be used, "Piano-vocal score" is preferred.

c. "Voice score," for editions of the voice parts, in score, without the accompaniment.

Arrangements of the work for piano alone are treated as arrangements. (See 9:2 J above.)

The last element in these conventional titles is the name of the language of the text, except that masses in Latin only have no language specification. This element is separated from the preceding one by a period. If there are two or more languages they are named in alphabetical order, except that English, if one of the languages, is always given first. If Latin is one of the languages in the conventional title of a mass, it is given last.

> ₁Lohengrin. German₁
> ₁Lohengrin. Piano-vocal score. German & Italian₁
> ₁Lohengrin. Libretto. English & German₁
> ₁The Messiah. Libretto. English & Dutch₁
> ₁Mass, op. 17, D major. Piano-vocal score₁
> ₁Mass, op. 17, D major. Piano-vocal score. Swedish & Latin₁

2. *Masses.* Masses which can be satisfactorily distinguished by such identifying elements as opus number, serial number, or key, have as conventional title the word "Mass," followed, after a comma, by the identifying elements. (See 9:2 E 1–3.) The conventional titles for other masses are formulated according to the general rules. (See 9:2 A and 9:2 C 2.)

---

[9] For comparable publications of the words of a song, "Text" is used.

Beethoven, Ludwig van, 1770–1827.
[Mass, op. 123, D major]
Missa solemnis in D, for four solo voices ...   Op. 123.

Yon, Pietro Alessandro, 1886–1943.
[Missa eucharistica]
Missa eucharistica for S. A. T. B. or S. T. T. B. with accompaniment of organ.

Korman, James A
[Easter mass]
Easter mass (including familiar Eastern church melodies)

Tit!es including a phrase naming a person honored are abridged to omit such parts of the phrase as "in honor of," "in honorem," etc.

Singenberger, John Baptist, 1848–1924.
[Missa, S. Caeciliae ...]
Missa in honorem S. Caeciliae.

3. *Trio-sonatas.* An exception to the rule of giving preference to the title of the original edition is made in the case of trio-sonatas (works of the seventeenth and eighteenth centuries for two melody instruments and continuo) which, in their original editions, are termed "Sonatas," "Trios," or some combination of these two words, such as "Sonate a tre," "Sonates en trio," etc. A work called "Trio" on the title page may have the caption "Sonata." Contemporaneous editions of the same set frequently vary as to title. Below are listed four contemporaneous editions of trio-sonatas by Gaetano Pugnani as an example.

> Sei trio ...   Opera prima ...   [176–?]
> Six sonatas ...   Opera 1 ...   [176–?]
> Six sonatas ...   Opera secunda ...   [1765?]
> Six trios ...   Opera 9 ...   [1771?]

Since such variations are felt to be more fortuitous than significant, all such works are arbitrarily entered under the modern term for this genre, "Trio-sonatas." It is to be noted, however, that this is done only in the cases where the original title is simply "Trio," "Sonata a tre" or some form thereof. A "Sonata da camera" for two melody instruments and continuo, for example, is not so treated.

9:3. TRANSCRIPTION OF TITLE PAGE

Music title pages frequently do not have the distinctive character of title pages of literary works; the title page may have only a listing of some of the composer's works, or of works of the same type by other composers; the work in hand may appear as one of many items, usually briefly listed. In these cases another source having fuller information, such as the caption or cover, is more satisfactory as the basis of the description. In case of doubt, however, the title page is preferred.

Medium of performance, serial and opus numbers, and key are included after

the transcription of the title if they appear on the title page or title page substitute, even though they may have been stated in the conventional title.

In cataloging works with a title page in two or more languages (see 3:5 B) the language of the first title is given preference in recording in the body of the entry all data other than the title, if it corresponds with the language of the imprint. If data other than the title are to be given in two or more languages, all the data in one language precede that in another.

9:4. IMPRINT

The treatment of imprint in music is, with the qualifications noted below, the same as that for literary works. (See 3:10–3:13.)

A. *Additional publisher named.* If the application of the rule for describing a work with more than one place and publisher (see 3:10) results in the omission of the name of the publisher whose plate number appears on the work, an exception is made and this name is also included in the imprint. (See also paragraph C below.)

B. *Early American imprints.* Full imprint is given for music published in the United States through 1865 because these are rare publications, copies and issues of which can often be distinguished only by a comparison of publishers' addresses. Such imprints (place, publisher, printer, etc., and date) are transcribed exactly from the title page, following the order and punctuation, but not necessarily the capitalization of the work, and including addresses of printers and publishers, copyright notice, royal privilege, price, etc. The date is given in roman numerals if so printed on the title page. Omissions may be made from exceptionally long imprints and be represented by the standard mark of omission, three dots.

C. *Supplied date.* It must be borne in mind that much of the music which passes through the hands of the cataloger will not be of first issue. The one large trade bibliography, Hofmeister, *Handbuch der musikalischen Literatur*, usually lists only a given publisher's first issues, and in using it care should be taken to avoid dating a reissue as a first issue.

D. *Plate numbers and publishers' numbers.* For music which does not bear a publication, printing or copyright date, a plate number or publisher's number, if available, is added immediately after the supplied imprint date, for its value in identifying copies and comparing editions. The plate number appears at the foot of each page of most engraved music, and may also appear on the title page. If the number appears only on the title page it is designated as the "publisher's number." If both plate and publisher's numbers appear on the work, the latter is ignored. If an additional number, corresponding to the total number of pages or plates, follows the plate number (often after a dash) it is omitted in recording the plate number.

The number is given without brackets. It is designated "Pl. no." or "Pub. no." and is copied exactly as it appears: letters, figures, and punctuation.

London, Stainer & Bell ₍1931₎ Pl. no. S. & B. 408ᵃ.
Leipzig, Universal-Edition ₍1922₎ Pub. no. 6139.

In the case of a collection or work in several volumes, inclusive numbers are given if they are consecutive, individual numbers if not. If there are many numbers (generally more than three) the smallest and the largest are given, separated by a diagonal line. Letters preceding the numbers are transcribed only before the first number, letters following the numbers are transcribed only after the last number, but letters preceding *and* following the numbers are transcribed in conjunction with each number.

B. & H. 8797–8806.
B. M. Co. 10162, 10261, 10311.
6201/9935.
      (*The complete set of numbers is 6201, 6654, 7006, 7212, 7635, 7788, 8847, 9158, 8664, 9935.*)
9674–9676 H. L.
R. 10150 E.–R. 10155 E.

If the plate number is not that of a publisher named in the imprint, the original publisher, if easily ascertainable, is identified in a note.

Paris, Lemoine ₍18—₎ Pl. no. B. et Cie 4520.
Reissued from Brandus plates.

If the original publisher is not easily ascertainable and the plate number does not include the initial of his name, it is omitted from this position and the circumstance explained in a note.

Pl. no. 57 of a previous publisher.

9:5. COLLATION

Music which is not described as score and/or parts (such as music for a solo instrument, songs, hymnals, etc.) follows the rules for collation of other monographic or serial publications.

A. *Works consisting of score only.* Scores are specified as such in the collation, unless this term appears in English in the conventional title or in the body of the entry. Close score, condensed score, piano-conductor score, and miniature score [10] are likewise specified in the collation. Following the term for the score, the paging is stated within parentheses. Text preceding or following the music is not brought out in the collation unless it is separately paged, in which case the paging is given in the usual manner preceding or following the section indicating the score and its paging. When the score is a facsimile the abbreviation "facsim." and a colon precede the term for the score.

---

[10] This term is used for all full scores of less than 21 cm. height. It may be used for full scores of greater height provided they are in a format too small to serve as a conductor's score.

score (37 p.)
23 p., facsim.: score (133 p.), 8 p.

Shepherd, Arthur, 1880–

₍The city in the sea. Piano-vocal score. English₎
The city in the sea, poem for orchestra, chorus of mixed
voices, and baritone solo, to words by Bliss Carman. Boston,
Boston Music Co. ₍°1913₎

61 p.   27 cm.

B. *Works consisting of parts or score and parts.* Whenever the music cataloged
consists of or includes musical parts for performance, this fact is shown in the
collation by the word "parts." The number of parts is not stated, in order to
make the catalog entries more useful to other libraries which may follow a different
method of counting parts or which may have a different number of parts. A
blank space which may be used to record the number best suited to the practice
and particular needs of an individual library, is left before the word if it is used
in the plural.

Villa-Lobos, Heitor.

₍Quartet, strings, no. 5₎
String quartet 5. ₍New York₎ Associated Music Publishers
₍1948₎

parts.   33 cm.

If the work consists of score and parts, the presence of parts is shown after the
collation of the score, following the word "and."

score (45 p.) and   parts.
score (2 v.) and   parts.
score (23 p.), piano-conductor score (8 p.) and   parts.
score and part (5 p.) and   parts.
        (*The trombone part was printed on p. 5.   Had it been printed on an unnumbered
        leaf, the collation would have read: score (4 p.) and   parts.*)
condensed score (8 p.) and   parts.

Further description, such as illustrations or a variation in size, is included with
that part of the collation to which it applies.

score (27 p.   port.) and part.
miniature score (63 p.)   20 cm.   and   parts.   32 cm.
score (128 p.) and part (₍129₎–191 p.)

C. *Works for two pianos.* Works for two pianos may be published as a single
score (of which two copies are necessary for performance), as a set consisting of
two scores, as one score and one part, or as two parts. These are described,
respectively, as follows:

1. *One score.*

Konzert, A dur, für Klavier und Orchester, mit Begleitung
eines zweiten Klaviers ...

score (51 p.)   30 cm.

If the library has the second copy necessary for performance, the following note is added.

— —— Copy 2.

2. *Two scores.*

Scherzo for two pianos, four hands ...
2 scores (21 p. each) 30 cm.

3. *One score and one part.*

Drei Klavier-Quartette ... hrsg. für 2 Klaviere ...
score (83 p.) and part. 34 cm.

4. *Two parts.*

Suite for two pianos ...
2 parts. 30 cm.

9:6. NOTES

Additional information necessary in the catalog entry may be given as notes. Listed below in the order in which they should appear on the card are the various types of notes together with the procedures which are followed when the latter are peculiar to music and with references to other sections of these rules when the situation is the same as with other types of works.

A. *Series.* Collective titles such as "Tänze für das Orchester von Josef Strauss," and "Compositions célèbres de Saint-Saens," appearing on stock title pages, are not considered series. These titles are generally ignored. (See also 3:16.)

B. *Species.* If the item to be cataloged does not name the species to which it belongs (e. g., opera in 2 acts, lyric drama, song, etc.) and if the cataloger can define it, this information is given as the first supplementary note in the catalog entry.

C. *Medium of performance.* If not specifically stated in the conventional title or if included only in the body of the entry in a language other than English (unless cognate words make the specification unnecessary) the medium of the work in hand, and the original medium if the work in hand is an arrangement, are noted. If the work is for solo instruments, all are named if there are not more than eleven. Instruments, including alternative instruments, and voices are listed in the order of the score (excepting that voices are named first) and are given in English unless there is no precise English equivalent. The key of wind instruments is not given.

If the work is for orchestra, the instruments involved are not listed. If, however, the work is for orchestra and a solo instrument, the latter is named. In ensemble vocal music the appropriate term is followed by a parenthetical statement of the component voice parts, using the abbreviations S for soprano, Mz for mezzosoprano, A for alto, T for tenor, Bar for baritone, and B for bass, repeating the abbreviation if necessary to indicate the number of parts.

92

For voice and piano.
For chorus (TTB) and keyboard instrument.
For 2 violins and violoncello.
For alto saxophone and piano; originally for piano.
For orchestra.
For solo voices (SATB), chorus (SSATB) and orchestra.
For soprano and orchestra.
For violin and orchestra; originally for violin and piano.
For piano, 4 hands.
Arranged for guitar.

If the collation or conventional title description of the score and parts and statements appearing on the title page of the work present a discrepancy, or if they are otherwise inadequate, supplementary information is noted, combined with the information relating to the medium of performance.

For 4 clarinets with alternative parts for alto and bass clarinets.
Part for piano only.
Score (violin and piano) and part for viola.
  (Title page reads: Viola and piano.)

For choral music before 1600 the voices are named in the language of the work being cataloged.

For superius, contratenor, tenor and bassus.

For composite volumes or sets of music, the note concerning medium of performance should be descriptive of the work as a whole; if the contents are too miscellaneous to make such a note possible, it is omitted.

For 5–8 instruments.
For 3–5 stringed instruments.
For 1–3 voices and piano.

D. *Text: language, authors, etc.* Following the note on medium of performance, either in the same paragraph or as a separate note, the language of the text is indicated if it is not that of the title page. If the text is in more than one language, all are named in the order in which they appear in the work. Masses in Latin have no language specification.

For voice and piano; French and English words.
For baritone and orchestra; Russian, German and English words.
Part of the words in Latin, part in English.[11]
Words in Hebrew (transliterated)
Words in original language, with English translation.
Songs in languages other than English are accompanied by translations.

If the text is printed on preliminary pages of the work as well as with the music, this fact is disregarded unless the edition is one that might be used for the sake of the text.

English words, also printed as text on p. 3–7.
French and English words; French text also on p. vii–viii.

---

[11] Not used for single compositions.

Vocal works that are published without text and those for which the text is published without the music, or with only part of it, are so described. Works with arbitrary syllables as text are so described.

> Arranged for piano.
> Without the music.
> Without the music (composed and compiled by Arne)
> Includes the principal melodies (unacc.)
> The principal melodies arr. for piano: 8 p. at end.
> Arbitrary syllables as text.

The name of the author of the text of an opera, oratorio or other extended vocal work, together with the name of the author and title of a work on which the text may have been based, is included in the catalog entry; if necessary, in a note. It is not essential, however, to include this information for excerpts from such works. For vocal works of lesser extent, the author of the text is named only if the information is given in the copy in hand. A text from the Bible or from a church liturgy is also identified if the information is contained in the work in hand.[12] Translators are named only if the information appears in the work in hand.

> The libretto is by Arrigo Boito, based on Victor Hugo's Angelo.

E. *Notation.* Any notation that varies from the normal notation for a particular type of publication is mentioned in a note.

> Lute tablature and staff notation on opposite pages.
> Modern notation.
>   (*Used to describe the notation of a liturgical work that would normally be in plainsong notation.*)
> Plainsong notation.
> Tonic sol-fa notation.
> Melody in both staff and tonic-sol-fa notation.
> Shape-note notation.

F. *Duration of performance.* The duration of performance is stated in the catalog entry only if the information on the duration of the entire work is available in the work in hand. The statement is given in English in the form:

> Duration: 18 minutes, 15 seconds.
> Duration: about 1 hour, 10 minutes.

G. *Contents.* Although the general form of the contents note agrees with that used in describing other monographic publications, various special devices are used in the cataloging of music, as indicated below.

Opus numbers are included in the contents statement if they are necessary to identify the works named, and are easily ascertained.

> CONTENTS.—Sonata in D major [op. 6]—Three marches [op. 45]—Variations in C major [op. 23]—Variation in C major [op. 34]

---

[12] An added entry is not made for excerpts from the Bible or from liturgies since such settings can be brought together by subject headings or in a classed catalog.

Titles in the contents note for a collection of works in the same musical form may consist of conventional titles without the repetition of the name of the musical form.

> **Händel, Georg Friedrich,** 1685–1759.
> ₍Sonatas, flute and bass. Selections₎
> Sonatas for flute and piano, study version by Georges Barrère.
> Boston, Boston Music Co. ₍1944₎
>
> score and part. ports. 30 cm.
>
> CONTENTS.—**v. 1.** No. 1 (op. 1, no. 1b) E minor. No. 2 (op. 1, no. 2) G minor. No. 3 (op. 1, no. 5) G major. No. 4 (op. 1, no. 7) C major.— **v. 2.** No. 5 (op. 1, no. 11) F major. No. 6 (op. 1, no. 9) B minor. No. 7 (op. 1, no. 4) A minor. No. 8, A minor.

For a collection of songs having texts by various poets, the names of the poets may be shown in the contents note.

> CONTENTS.—The heart of England (Irene Gass)—June in Devon (Irene Gass)—Men of England (Thomas Campbell)—Tewksbury Road (John Masefield)

If the titles in a collection of songs appear in two languages and if it is considered desirable to include both in the contents note, the second title is enclosed in parentheses.

> CONTENTS.—Liebesdurchbruch (Love triumphant)—Tod in Aehren (The dying soldier)—Die Nachtigall (The nightingale)—Die Tote (To her I lost)—Sommermittag (Midsummer day)

10. Facsimiles, Photocopies and Microfilms

10:1. INTRODUCTION

Photographic reproductions of books or other works include facsimile editions,[1] photostats or other photocopies, and microfilm copies. The objective in cataloging each of these types is the same: to identify and characterize the work that has been reproduced, and to describe the physical object in hand to the extent necessary for its use. To this end the rules for cataloging monographs, serials, music, etc., are applicable to the cataloging of photographic reproductions of these respective works, with certain exceptions and additions noted below.

In each case the location of the specific copy that has been reproduced is noted if the facts are known.[2] The statement can generally be quoted from the work.

A single catalog entry may describe a set of works, or a serial publication, consisting of a combination of original and reproduced volumes. In this case the form of the reproduced volumes is simply noted.

> Vol. 1, no. 1 is a photocopy (negative)
> Vol. 15 (1942) photographic copy "reproduced and distributed in the public interest by the Alien Property Custodian."
> 1933 report, microfilm copy (negative) made in 1943 by the Library of Congress.

10:2. FACSIMILES

A. *Choice of title page.* Facsimile editions of monographic and serial publications generally have a title page or title page substitute embracing the entire work, in addition to the facsimile of the original title page. This comprehensive title page is used as the basis of the catalog entry for either a monographic or a serial publication. If the wording of the original title differs from that of the reproduction, the title page data that are included in the body of a catalog entry are noted.

> Original title page reads: The comicall historie of Alphonsus, King of Aragon ... Made by R. G. London, Brinted [sic] by T. Creede, 1599.

If a modern title page, but no other new matter, such as an introduction, is added to a facsimile, the original title page may be selected as the basis of the catalog entry to facilitate the arrangement of the various entries for the work.

---

[1] Type-facsimiles, or facsimile reprints, are handled according to the rules for cataloging true facsimiles except that the word "reprint" is substituted for "facsim." in the collation.

[2] Exception is made for American academic dissertations because it is common knowledge that the original copy will be found in the library of the university to which the dissertation was presented in partial fulfillment of the requirements for a degree.

If the only title page is the reproduction of the original one, this necessarily becomes the basis of the catalog entry.

B. *Imprint.* If the original title page is used as the basis of the description, the original imprint is included in the body of the entry; it is followed, however, by the supplied imprint of the reproduction.

London, 1783. ₁London, N. Douglas, 1926₁

C. *Collation.* The pagination consists of the paging of the facsimile and the paging of new matter that has been added. The former is set off and designated as "facsim." Parentheses are used to enclose the pagination of the facsimile if new matter follows it in the work.

15 p., facsim.: 28 p.
facsim. (28 p.), 15 p.

Illustrative matter within the facsimile is indicated with its pagination. Size is indicated as for other material.

₁4₁ l., facsim. (28 p. map), 15 p. 27 cm.

D. *Notes.* Any additional information that needs to be given about the work or its reproduction is presented in supplementary notes. If there are several notes referring to the reproduction they are grouped together, preferably in a single paragraph.

Southern, John, *fl.* 1584.

Pandora. Reproduced from the original ed., 1584, with a bibliographical note by George B. Parks. New York, Columbia University Press, 1938.

₁5₁ l., facsim.: ₁31₁ p. 20 cm. (Facsimile Text Society. Publication no. 43)

Reproduction of the Huntington Library copy of the original ed., with t. p. reading: Pandora, the musyque of the bcautie, of his mistresse Diana. Composed by John Soowthern, gentleman. Imprinted at London for Thomas Hackette and are to be solde at his shoppe in Lumbert Streete vnder the Popes Head, 1584.

The reproduction includes Richard Heber's manuscript notes on flyleaves of the Huntington copy.

Galilei, Vincenzo, *d.* 1591.

Discorso intorno all' opere di messer Gioseffo Zarlino da Chioggia, et altri importanti particolari attenenti alla musica. Fiorenza, G. Marescotti, 1589. ₁Milano, Bollettino bibliografico musicale, 1933₁

₁1₁ l., facsim. (134 p.), ₁1₁ l. 15 cm. (Collezione di trattati e musiche antiche edite in fac-simile)

"Edizione di 150 esemplari."

Title vignette: device of Marescotti.

Added t. p. (with series title and imprint of the reproduction): Discorso intorno alle opere di Gioseffo Zarlino et altri importanti particolari attenenti alla musica. Venezia ₁sic₁ MDLXXXIX.

Diario pinciano; primer periódico de Valladolid (1787–88)
Reproducción facsímil hecha por la Academia de Bellas Artes

de Valladolid con prólogo de Narciso Alonso Cortés, presidente de la misma. ₁Valladolid, Impr. Castellana, 1933₁

xxxi p., facsim.: 8, 360 p. 23 cm.

Reproduction of no. 1-34 (Feb. 7-Oct. 24, 1787) of the weekly periodical which was published Feb. 7, 1787–June 25, 1788, and edited by J. M. Beristain. "Plan del Diario pinciano" precedes the first number.

El Eco de los Andes. Mendoza, 1943.

₁60₁ p., facsim.: 61 no. 29 cm.

At head of title: Universidad Nacional de Cuyo. Instituto de Investigaciones Históricas.

Facsimile reproduction of a weekly periodical published in Mendoza, Sept. 23, 1824–Dec. 25, 1825 (except Sept. 12 to Oct. 8, 1825, inclusive, when publication was suspended) and edited by J. G. Godoy, F. de B. Correas, J. L. Calle and J. M. Salinas. No. 28, 41, 50–51, 53, 56 and 58 are wanting in the reproduction.

Primicias de la cultura de Quito. Reedición de la "Unión Nacional de Periodistas del Ecuador," en homenaje al egregio polemista y hombre de ciencia, Dr. Francisco Javier Eugenio Santa Cruz y Espejo, en el cxcvii aniversario de su nacimiento. Quito, Ecuador ₁Impr. del Mtrio. de Gobierno₁ 1944.

93 p. port., facsim. 22 cm.

A reissue of the biweekly periodical published Jan. 5–Mar. 29, 1792 (7 no.) and edited by F. J. E. Santa Cruz y Espejo.

10:3. PHOTOCOPIES

If photostats and other photocopies have additional title pages or other new matter, they are cataloged according to the rules for facsimile editions. Otherwise, the catalog entry is prepared as if the work in hand were the original and a note is added to describe the form of the item in hand and to give any other data relating to it.

Photocopy (negative) made in 1947 by the New York Public Library.

10:4. MICROFILMS

A publication on microfilm may be merely a photographic reproduction of a previously published work or of a manuscript or it may itself be a form of publication with the producer playing the role of publisher. The former situation is assumed to be the case unless specific information to the contrary is available.

A. *Imprint.* The imprint given in the catalog entry is that which would be used in describing the original unless the work was previously unpublished and it is known that the microfilm is a publication.

B. *Collation.* The normal collation position in the catalog entry is used for the number of reels if more than one. No collation is given for a film that is complete on one reel.

The collation of the material reproduced is given as a supplementary note; if it cannot be ascertained easily, the length of the film in feet is noted instead.

C. Description of the film. The first supplementary note after the series note reveals the fact that the work is a microfilm reproduction, and whether it is positive or negative; if it is not 35 mm. film, the width in millimeters is added.

Thein, Adelaide Eve, 1890–

The religion of William Cowper; an attempt to distinguish between his obsession and his creed. [Ann Arbor] 1940.

Microfilm copy of typewritten manuscript. Made in 1943 by University Microfilms (Publication no. 577) Positive.
Collation of the original: xxxvii, 442 l.
Thesis--University of Michigan.
Abstracted in Microfilm abstracts, v. 5 (1943) no. 1, p. 24.
Bibliography: leaves 434–442.

Logsdon, Richard Henry, 1912–

The instructional literature of sociology and the administration of college library book collections. Chicago ¡University of Chicago Library, Dept. of Photographic Reproduction¡ 1947.

Microfilm copy of typewritten manuscript. Positive.
Collation of the original: vi, 100 l. tables.
Thesis—University of Chicago.

Reinoso, Pedro.

Advertencias de declinaciones, y de todo genero de tiempos, con otros rudimentos de la grammatica. Mexico, Impr. Nueva Plantiniana de D. Fernandez de Leon, 1710.

Microfilm copy, made in 1941, of the original in the Medina collection, Biblioteca Nacional de Santiago de Chile. Positive.
Negative film in Brown University Library.
Collation of the original, as determined from the film: ¡80¡ p.
Medina, La imprenta en Mexico. 2265.

11. Incunabula

11:1. INTRODUCTION

Detailed descriptions of incunabula can generally be found in one or more of the following reference works:

Hain, L. Repertorium bibliographicum, with its supplements: W. A. Copinger. Supplement to Hain's Repertorium bibliographicum, and D. Reichling. Appendices ad Hainii-Copingeri Repertorium bibliographicum.

British Museum. Catalogue of books printed in the xvth century.

Gesamtkatalog der Wiegendrucke, hrsg. von uer Kommission für den Gesamtkatalog der Wiegendrucke.

Pellechet, M. L. C. Catalogue générale des incunables des bibliothèques publiques de France.

Polain, L. Catalogue des livres imprimés au quinzième siècle des bibliothèques de Belgique.

and in other catalogs of incunabula. Such descriptions need not be repeated on the cards if they fit the work being cataloged. Instead, reference is made to the best description found, making the catalog entry relatively brief and simple.[1]

Because most incunabula were issued without title pages and many without a definite title, the items given in the body of the entry are presented in a conventional form which will enable the user to identify the work easily.

11:2. TITLE

The shortened or conventional form of title found in a competent authority is used, without brackets, as the title of a given incunabulum. This title should be in the language in which the book was first published, except that the Latin title is always used for Greek works. If the title is not found in such an authority, it is taken from the work, whether it appears as a title or as a descriptive statement in the colophon or text.

If a separately published part of a work is known under its own title, the conventional form of this title is used and the relation to the main work stated in a note. If it is known only as a part of the larger work, the conventional form of title of the latter is used, followed by the necessary qualification; e. g., Liber 1–13,

---

[1] These rules for a simplified cataloging of incunabula are based on the assumption that the Library will have other records of its incunabula (either in a special sheet-catalog or in other form) where peculiarities of the copy in hand and variations from the printed descriptions will be registered with some minuteness. At the Library of Congress, additional details not of primary importance to other libraries are recorded in the Official Catalog.

Selections, Pars aestivalis, etc. If the qualification cannot be stated concisely it is omitted from this position and stated in a note.

11:3. INDICATION OF LANGUAGE

The title is followed by the name of the language of the text if this differs from the language of the conventional form of title or if the title does not indicate the language.

11:4. IMPRINT

The place of printing is given in the form used as catalog entry, followed, in parentheses, by the form used in the book if notably different.

> Leyden (Lugduni Batavorum)

The name of the printer, or publisher and printer if both are known, is given in the form used in the British Museum *Catalogue of Books Printed in the xvth Century,* or in Proctor's *Index.*[2] The same form is used in Stillwell's census.[3] Such designations as "Printer of the 1481 Legenda aurea" may be used.

If available, the exact date of publication, including day and month, is given according to modern style of chronology. If the work gives the date in the form of the Roman, ecclesiastical or other calendar, this form is added, enclosed in parentheses.[4]

> Aug. 21 (xii Kal. Sept.) 1473.
> Aug. 9 (in vigilia S. Laurentii Martyris) 1492.

For a work dated according to a usage in which the year does not begin with January 1, the date as given in the work is followed by the year according to the Roman calendar.

> Mar. 3, 1483/84.

If the work is undated, an approximate date showing the degree of approximation is given.

> [1492?]
> [ca. 1492]
> [not after Aug. 21, 1492]

The imprint, or any part of it that is not to be found in a perfect copy of the work, is supplied in brackets. If the place or date of publication cannot be supplied, the abbreviations "n. p." or "n. d." are used.

[2] Proctor, R. *An Index to the Early Printed Books in the British Museum* ... London, 1898–1903. 2 v.

[3] Stillwell, M. B. *Incunabula in American Libraries; a Second Census of Fifteenth Century Books* ... New York, Bibliographical Society of America, 1940.

[4] The date according to modern usage is obtained from H. Grotefend's *Taschenbuch der Zeitrechnung des deutschen Mittelalters und der Neuzeit,* 1898 (8. Aufl., 1941) or F. R. Goff's *The Dates in Certain German Incunabula* (*in* Papers of the Bibliographical Society of America, v. 34 (1940) p. 17–67)

11:5. COLLATION

The collation consists of the total number of leaves of a complete copy, including blank leaves, brief description of illustrations, and size. For works of more than one volume, the number of volumes and the number of leaves are given. The number of leaves is enclosed in brackets if the foliation is not printed in the book. Blank leaves are specified here, and also the lacunae of the copy in hand if they can be listed briefly. (See also 11:6 E.)

> [4], 12, 551, [1] l.
> [5], ii–cxv, [1] l., the last blank.
> [16], 144, [2] l.; the first prelim. leaf (blank) and leaves 21–22 wanting.
> [1], ii–clvii (i. e. cliv), [4] l.
> 2 v. ([242], [239] l.)

Illustrations are always mentioned. They are described with the fullness and detail provided by rule 3:14 C, with specification whether the illustrations are woodcuts or metal engravings. If borders, printers' and publishers' devices, noteworthy initials, and head and tail pieces can be mentioned briefly, their presence is noted in the collation statement. (See also 11:6 below.)

> woodcuts: 1 illus., 2 diagrs.
> woodcut: illus.
> woodcuts: illus., initials, publisher's and printer's devices.
> metal cuts: illus., borders.
> illus.: 13 metal cuts, 24 woodcuts.

Size is indicated both by the fold of the paper (i. e., f°, 4°, 8°, etc.) and by the height or height and width of the binding (see 3:14 D) in centimeters, exact to the nearest millimeter.

> 4°. 27.5 cm.

11: 6. NOTES

In addition to the types of notes used in cataloging books printed after 1500 the following are used in cataloging incunabula.

A. *Title of the work in hand.* If the edition in hand has a title page, or a title differing notably from the conventional form of title, the title is quoted as the first note.

> Leaf [1ª] (t. p.): The descrypcyon of Englonde.
> Leaf [76ᵇ]: Thus endeth thys book of The dictes and notable wyse sayenges of the phylosophers.
> Leaf cciª (colophon): Cy finist Le mirouer de la redēption de lumaine lignaige ...
> Leaf [2ª]: Incipit Speculum vite Cristi ... The booke that is cleped The myrroure of the blessyd lyf of Jhesu Cryste.

B. *Bibliographical references.* Reference is made to one or more descriptions of the book in hand with a view to excellence or special relevance. If the best description is in a rare or inaccessible work, a second reference to a better known work is added as an aid in identification. The descriptions contained in Hain, (with Copinger's *Supplement* and Reichling's *Appendices*) and the *Gesamtkatalog der Wiegendrucke* are always noted. Special attention is called to the description used for significant data too profuse to be repeated on the catalog card. The references are given in a brief but unmistakable form. Variation presented by the book in hand from the description cited is noted (but only major variations are described) except that variations from Hain, or Hain-Copinger, are not noted if a more adequate reference identifying the work with the same Hain number is cited.

> Hain. Repertorium (with Reichling's Appendices) 6741 (variations from Reichling); Gesamtkat. d. Wiegendr. 9101.
>
> Hain. Repertorium *14582; Brit. Mus. Cat. (xv cent.) ɪɪ, p. 346 (IB. 5874); Schramm. Bilderschmuck d. Frühdr., v. 4, p. 10. 50, and illus.
>
> Hain. Repertorium (with Copinger's Supplement) 4952; La Marche. La chevalier délibéré. Washington, 1946 (facsim. ed. of this copy with Introd. and Note)
>
> Reichling. Appendices, 1514 (variations); Perrin. Ital. book-illus., 90.
>
> Hain. Repertorium (with Copinger's Supplement) 11447; Thiébaud. Bibl. des ouvrages franç. sur la chasse, col. 388–395 (variation; see also for provenance of this copy)

C. *Elaboration of collation.* Foliation or illustrations that cannot be adequately described in the collation statement are further described in notes. Account of signatures is given, as in books printed after 1500, if the leaves or pages are unnumbered or irregular in their numbering, and if the account is not given in a bibliographical source cited. Color printing is noted. Number of columns, number of lines, type measurements, etc., are given if essential for identification and if no account is found in a bibliographical source.

> The illustrations are copper engravings.
> Woodcuts on leaves ₍10ᵇ₎ and ₍21ᵇ₎ signed: b.
> Printed in black and red.
> Signatures: a–v⁸, x⁶.
> Type 96 G.
> *(Printer identified through type.)*

D. *Contents.* Contents or partial contents are noted informally following the form of the data in the work being cataloged or giving the catalog entry form of the author's name and the conventional form of the title of each work contained, whichever is simpler.

E. *Description of the copy in hand.* The peculiarities of the copy in hand, including note of imperfections other than those given in the collation statement, are described in the last note or group of notes. The data covered include the following: rubrication, illumination, manuscript additions, binding (if contemporary or otherwise notable) and provenance.

> L. C. copy imperfect: the first 2 leaves in facsim., apparently printed on blank leaves ₍12₎ and ₍13₎ (b₄ and c₁); ₍12₎ and ₍13₎ replaced by modern leaves; last blank leaf (S₈) wanting.
> Signatures I₅₋₆ incorrectly bound between h₂ and h₄.

Initials and paragraph marks supplied in red.

On vellum.   Illustrations and part of illustrated borders hand-colored.
Rubricated in gold, red and blue.

Old gilt red morocco.

Contemporary doeskin over boards; clasp.   Stamp: Château de la
Roche Guyon, Bibliothèque.

Bookplates of Michel de Leon and A. E. Newton.

Inscription on inside of front cover: Theodorinis ab Engelsperg.

. F. *Unrecorded incunabula*.   Titles which cannot be found described in some
reference work are not given more detailed bibliographical description than
other incunabula unless there is reason to believe that this is necessary for the
identification of the work; e. g., if the title and imprint data are supplied by the
cataloger.   The source of such data (incipit, closing words, colophon, or type
face, etc.) is noted.   (See 11: 6 C.)

12. History Cards

A statement is prepared for the catalog to show the following information about corporate bodies if any of the facts are ascertained and if the recording of them will help the user of the catalog or catalogers in other libraries:

a. Date of founding.
b. Date of incorporation.
c. Changes of name.
d. Affiliation or union with other bodies.
e. Date of dissolution.

The information is presented as concisely as possible, in narrative style, under the form of the heading that is adopted for entry of the publications of the body.

National Society for Crippled Children and Adults.

Organized Oct. 28, 1921 as the National Society for Crippled Children. Name changed Feb. 5, 1922 to International Society for Crippled Children; incorporated on April 1, 1929. On Dec. 22, 1938 the name was changed to National Society for Crippled Children of the United States of America, and on Feb. 9, 1945 to National Society for Crippled Children and Adults.

Augustana College, *Sioux Falls, S. D.*

Created in 1918 as Augustana College and Normal School by the merger of the Augustana College at Canton, S. D., and the Lutheran Normal School at Sioux Falls. Later called Augustana College.

Similar information is prepared for names of places that are used as headings in the catalog if the scope of the territory requires definition.

West Florida.

The northern coast of the Gulf of Mexico between the Mississippi and Apalachicola Rivers. Formed part of Louisiana until 1763 when French possessions east of the Mississippi were ceded to Great Britain. British West Florida was organized in 1763, with line of 31° as northern boundary, changed in 1767 to 32°28'. Conquered by Spain in 1780, its northern boundary was in dispute until 1791, when 31° was agreed upon, and the section thereby gained by the U. S. between 31° and 32°28' became Mississippi Territory. In 1810–11 the western section, or Baton Rouge district, of Spanish West Florida revolted from Spain and was joined to Louisiana; in 1812, the middle section, or Mobile district, was annexed to Mississippi Territory; and in 1819 the eastern section with the whole of East Florida was sold by Spain to the U. S., forming the present State of Florida.

Appendix I. Glossary

Supplementary to the *A. L. A. Glossary of Library Terms*

Catalogers have requested that a full glossary of the terms used in these rules be included with the rules. A study of the terms that would be included in such a glossary and of the scope of the *A. L. A. Glossary of Library Terms* (Chicago, 1943) demonstrated that with few exceptions the two lists would overlap. Most of the definitions of cataloging terms that are to be found in the *A. L. A. Glossary* were reprinted, some with minor alterations, from the preliminary American second edition of the *A. L. A. Catalog Rules*. Since these definitions are available, it has not seemed expedient to reprint them with the cataloging rules. The following list of terms is limited, therefore, to terms that do not appear in the *A. L. A. Glossary* and those for which definitions other than those given in the *A. L. A. Glossary* are necessary for these rules. In certain cases, special usage at the Library of Congress has made a corresponding special definition desirable.

ANALYTICAL ENTRY. An entry for a part of a work or series of works for which another, comprehensive, entry is made.

APPENDIX. *See* the definition in the *A. L. A. Glossary of Library Terms* but qualify it by adding: if so called by the publisher or author.

AUTHOR-TITLE ADDED ENTRY. An added entry consisting of the author and title of a work which is contained in or related to the work represented by the main entry, such as the original work upon which an adaptation is based.

CONVENTIONAL TITLE. A filing title constructed according to fixed rules to present in a systematic order the catalog entries for the various forms of a musical work.

COPYRIGHT DATE. The date of copyright as recorded in the Copyright Office, and (as a rule) as given in the book on the back of the title page.

COVER TITLE. The title printed on the original covers of a book or pamphlet, or lettered or stamped on the publisher's binding, as distinguished from the title lettered on the cover of a particular copy by a binder.

FILING TITLE. The title by which a work that has appeared under varying titles is filed. (*See also* Conventional title.) The phrase "filing title" is also used at the Library of Congress to refer to such filing media as "Works," "Selections," "Correspondence," etc., which are used so that such works will be arranged systematically in the catalog.

MINIATURE BOOK. A book that is ten centimeters or less in height.

ORGAN-VOCAL SCORE. A score of a work for chorus and/or solo voices and organ, the accompaniment being a reduction of the music originally composed for an instrumental ensemble.

PERIODICAL. *See* the definition in the *A. L. A. Glossary of Library Terms*, but qualify it as follows: A publication, *generally* with a distinctive title, intended [etc.]

PIANO-VOCAL SCORE. A score of a work for chorus and/or solo voices and piano, the accompaniment being a reduction of the music originally composed for an instrumental ensemble.

REPRESENTATIVE FRACTION. The representative fraction is the ratio between distance measured on a map and the corresponding distance on the ground. Thus a map on the scale of 1 inch to 1 mile has a representative fraction of 1:63,360, there being 63,360 inches in a mile.

SERIAL. A publication issued in successive parts, and, generally, intended to be continued indefinitely. "Serial" is a more specific term than "continuation" which includes serials, books or sets of books issued in parts, supplements to previously published works, and insert sheets for loose-leaf publications. Serials include periodicals, newspapers, annuals, and other sequences of non-monographic publications, and series, the separate parts of which appear from time to time under a collective title.

SERIES ENTRY. A catalog entry, under the name of the series as the heading, of a single work belonging to the series.

SERIES STATEMENT. The information on a publication which names the series to which it belongs and specifies its place in the series if the series is comprised of a numbered sequence of parts.

STANDARD TITLE. *See* Conventional title.

TITLE. Throughout these rules the second definition of title (i. e., in the narrow sense) appearing in the *A. L. A. Glossary of Library Terms* is used.

Appendix II. Capitalization

The rules for capitalization are those given in the United States Government Printing Office *Style Manual* (Rev. ed., Jan. 1945) with certain exceptions and additions. For English, only the exceptions and additions are included here. Capitalization in other languages is similar to that in English with exceptions specified in the *Style Manual* and below. The exceptions to English capitalization for the foreign languages in this list include the rules given in the corresponding sections of the *Style Manual*.

A. ENGLISH

1. *Titles of publications, papers, documents, acts, laws, etc.* The following is to be substituted for rule 17, p. 21–22:

In the titles of books, pamphlets, periodicals, documents, and other publications, legal cases, and works of art, the first word is capitalized. The capitalization of the other words in the title is governed by the other rules for capitalization. This rule applies also to the titles of parts of such works, but not to the words appendix, index, introduction, supplement, etc., referring to such a part, unless these parts have title pages of their own or exist in separate form.

> The outline of history.
> Address of President Roosevelt on unemployment relief.
> American journal of science.
> The Fourteenth amendment.
> The Magna carta.
> The United States *vs.* The bark Springbok and her cargo.
> The Reform bill.
> The Treaty of Ghent.

a. The first word of every title quoted and every alternative title introduced by "or" or its equivalent, is capitalized.

> An interpretation of The ring and the book.
> Selections from the Idylls of the king.
> Alexander's feast; or, The power of musique.

b. When one periodical absorbs or merges with another and incorporates its title with its own, the first word in the incorporated title is not capitalized as such.

> Illinois mining gazette and railway age

c. The first word of a title is not capitalized if it is preceded by dots, dashes, or other symbols indicating that the beginning of the phrase from which the title was derived has been omitted. The symbols of omission are transcribed as a part of the title. Dots occurring on the title page as a mark of elision are represented in the catalog entry by bold face periods.

... and master of none.
—— and the other Mary.

d. In titles used as main entries (except anonymous works which, theoretically, are only temporarily main entires) and the corresponding series notes, if the first word is an article, the word following it is capitalized. The article is also capitalized except when the title appears within a sentence written in the same language as the title, and is not enclosed within quotation marks.

> The Anatomical record.
> "Reprinted from the Anatomical record, vol. 88, Jan.–Mar. 1944."
> Separate from La Revista de derecho, jurisprudencia y administración.
> "... in the September 1946 issue of 'The Woman's press.' "

2. *Names of organized bodies.* The following is to be added as rule 6 b:

The expression indicating incorporation, or limited liability, appearing after the name of a firm or other body is not capitalized.

> incorporated, inc., limited, ltd.

3. *Religious terms.* The following examples are to be added to those given with rule 15:

> Father, Fathers (meaning church fathers), Nicene Fathers, Mother, Mother Superior, Saint, Bishop, Archbishop.

a. The word book when it refers to the entire Bible is capitalized.

> the Book, but the book of Proverbs

b. The first word of the names of special selections from the Bible that are commonly referred to under a specific head is capitalized.

> Beatitudes
> Sermon on the Mount
> Nunc dimittis
> Ten commandments
> Decalogue

c. The first word of the names of versions of the Bible is capitalized.

> Authorized version
> Revised version
> Septuagint
> Vulgate

4. *Titles of persons.* The caption "Title of a ruler or prince" in rule 16 a should have added: (including queens and princesses) The following section should be added:

Miscellaneous titles capitalized:

> Pope

a. Ordinal numbers used after names of sovereigns and popes to denote order of succession are capitalized.

> George the Sixth
> Pius the Eleventh

5. *Names in religion.* All pronouns, adjectives, and common nouns in names in religion are capitalized.

> Sister Mary of the Angels
> Father Raphael of Our Lady of Perpetual Help

6. *Peoples, races and tribes.* Names and epithets of peoples, races and tribes are capitalized.

> Negroes, Malay, Kafir, Aryans, Bushmen, Hottentots

7. *Prefixes.* Prefixes joined by a hyphen to a capitalized word are not themselves capitalized.

> ex-President Roosevelt
> pre-Cambrian
> trans-Siberian
> un-American

8. *Abbreviations.* In general, abbreviations follow the capitalization of the words abbreviated.

a. Abbreviations for degrees and honorary titles are capitalized. In printing, all letters are set in small capitals.

> PH. D., LL. D., LITT. .D., M. P., F. R. G. S.

b. Abbreviations of the names of eras are capitalized. In printing, all letters are set in small capitals.

> A. D., B. C., A. H.

9. *Roman numerals.* Roman numerals are written with small capital letters except those used in paging or in page references and those appearing in lower case in the title or in a quoted note. The roman L (50) when standing alone is always printed with a small capital letter to distinguish it from 1 (one).

10. *Imprints.* The first word in the statement of the publisher or printer in an imprint is capitalized; if the first word is an article, the second word is also capitalized.

11. *Collation.* Each item in the collation statement of illustrative matter is lower-cased.

> illus., ports., maps.

B. CZECH (Bohemian)

1. *Proper names and their derivatives.* When a geographic name consists of a distinctive word and a generic word, only the distinctive word is capitalized: *Tichý oceán.*

In names of streets, the first word only is capitalized: *U invalidovny; Na růžku,* unless another word is a derivative of a proper name: *Na Smetance.*

2. *Names of organized bodies.* In the names of corporate bodies, generally only the first word is capitalized: *Česká akademie věd a umění; Československá republika.*

Names of branches of schools, conservatories, universities, ministries and departments of government are not capitalized: *ministerstvo školství; závodní rada*

3. *Religious terms.* The word *svatý* (holy or saint) is lower-cased.

In the names of religious bodies, the first word only is capitalized: *Bratří čeští Milosrdní bratří.*

4. *Personal pronouns.* The personal pronoun *já* is lower-cased. The pronoun of formal address: *Ty, Tvůj, Tobě; Vy, Vám, Vás, Vás,* are capitalized.

C. DANISH. *See* SCANDINAVIAN LANGUAGES.

D. DUTCH

1. *Particles in names of persons.* The name particles *de, ten, van,* if not preceded by the Christian name, are capitalized.

2. *First words.* If the first word of a sentence is a single letter only, the word is lower-cased, and the next one is capitalized: *'s Avonds is het koud. 'k Weet niet wat hij zegt.*

If the first word of a sentence is the interjection *O,* the pronoun *U,* or a letter referring to a letter of the alphabet as such (*e. g.,* ABC) it is capitalized.

3. *Personal pronouns.* The first-person pronoun, *ik,* is not capitalized; the second-person pronouns *U, Uw,* and *Gij,* are generally capitalized in personal correspondence.

E. FRENCH

1. *Proper names and their derivatives.* Names of members of religious groups, sects, religious orders, political and other organizations, names of religions and languages are lower-cased: *les jésuites, les démocrates, le bouddhisme, l'anglais* (the English language). Adjectives derived from these names, from geographic names, and adjectives denoting nationality are lower-cased: *la religion catholique, la région alpine, le peuple français.* Nouns denoting nationality, however, are capitalized: *les Français.* A common noun used as a generic word in a geographic name is lower-cased: *la mer du Nord, l'île aux Oiseaux.*

2. *Particles in names of persons.* Prefixes of French names consisting of an article or contraction of a preposition and article are capitalized: *La Fontaine, Du Cange.*

3. *Names of organized bodies.* In the names of corporate bodies, the first word, any adjective preceding the first noun, the first noun, and all proper nouns are capitalized. Notable exceptions: *Société des Nations, Nations Unies.*

4. *Hyphenated names.* In hyphenated names, the nouns and adjectives are capitalized: *le Théâtre-Français.*

114

5. *Names of calendar divisions.* Names of days and months are lower-cased.

6. *Titles of persons.* Titles designating rank or office are lower-cased: *le roi, le ministre, le pape Leo x;* however, titles of address and titles of respectful address or reference are capitalized: *Monsieur, Mme Lafayette, Son Éminence, Sa Majesté le roi de France.* The word *saint (sainte, etc.)* is lower-cased when it refers exclusively to a person; it is otherwise capitalized: *saint Thomas More, la cathédrale Saint-Lambert, l'été de la Saint-Martin.*

7. *Personal pronouns.* The personal pronoun *je* is lower-cased.

8. *Miscellaneous.* The word *rue* and its synonyms are lower-cased, *rue de la Nation; avenue de l'Opéra.* The word *église,* when it indicates a building is lower-cased, *l'église Notre-Dame. L'Église,* when referring to the church as an institution, and *l'État,* when denoting the nation, are capitalized: *le Conseil d'État.*

F. GERMAN

1. All nouns and words used as nouns are capitalized: *das Geben; die Armen; das intime Du* (referring to the word *Du*).

2. Proper adjectives are lower-cased: *die deutsche Sprache.*

3. Adjectives derived from personal names are capitalized: *die Lutherische Übersetzung* (Luther's translation); but when used descriptively, lower-cased: *die lutherische Kirche* (the Lutheran Church); *ciceronische Beredsamkeit.*

4. Indeclinable adjectives derived from geographic names (ending in *er*) are capitalized: *Schweizer Ware; die Zürcher Bürger.*

5. The pronouns *Sie, Ihr* and *Ihnen* are capitalized, but not *ich.*

6. Pronouns used in direct address, and in salutations of letters are capitalized: *Du, Deine; Ihr, Euer; Sie, Ihr.*

7. Adjectives, pronouns, and numerals used as part of a name or title are capitalized: *Alexander der Grosse, das Schweizerische Konsulat, Seine Excellenz, Friedrich der Zweite, Bund der Technischen Angestellten und Beamten, der Erste der Klasse* (expressing rank) (See also b below.)

The categories below are not capitalized, and thus are covered by the statement that categories not specified follow the conventions in English. Nevertheless, for clarification, rule 1 that "all nouns and words used as nouns are capitalized," is supplemented by the following specifications:

a. Pronouns (see also 6 above): *jemand, ein jeder, der eine ... der andere, etwas anderes, die übrigen.*

b. Numerals (see also 7 above): *die beiden, alle drei, der vierte* (indicating numerical order).

c. Adverbs: *mittags, anfangs, morgen, montags, aufs neue, fürs erste, im voraus.*

d. Verbal phrases: *not tun, schuld sein, haushalten, preisgeben, teilhaben wundernehmen, außer acht lassen, zuteil werden, zumute sein.*

e. Adjectives modifying nouns that are implied if the noun has been expressed elsewhere in the same sentence: *Hier ist die beste Arbeit, dort die schlechteste.*

G. HUNGARIAN

Adjectives derived from proper names (*budapesti*), nouns denoting nationality (*az oroszok*), names of the months, of the days of the week, titles (including the title of nobility consisting of an adjectival term derived from place of origin etc., preceding the family name: *körmendi Frim Jakab*) and the personal pronoun *én* are lower-cased.

Pronouns and titles used in direct address are capitalized (*Maga, Felséges Uram*)

H. ITALIAN

1. *Proper names and their derivatives.* Names of members of religious groups, sects, religious orders, political and other organizations, names of religions and languages are lower-cased: *i protestanti, i benedettini, un democratico, il buddhismo, il francese* (the French language). Adjectives derived from these names, from geographical and personal names, and adjectives denoting nationality are lower-cased: *la religione cattolica, la flora alpina, il popolo italiano, la Società dantesca.* Nouns denoting nationality, however, are capitalized: *gl'Italiani.*

2. *Names of organized bodies.* In names of corporate bodies, generally only the first word, proper nouns, religious terms, and the word following an adjective denoting royal or pontifical privilege, are capitalized. Notable exceptions: *Società delle Nazioni, Nazioni Unite, Croce Rossa.*

3. *Names of calendar divisions.* Names of days and months are lower-cased.

4. *Names of centuries.* The names of centuries are capitalized: *il Cinquecento, il Seicento* (but: *il sedicesimo secolo*).

5. *Titles of persons.* Titles are lower-cased, except for ceremonious titles of respectful address or reference consisting of a possessive pronoun and a noun expressing an abstract quality: *signora, il signor Donati, il duca d'Aosta, Umberto I, re d'Italia. Sua Santità, Sua Altezza Reale il principe Umberto, le LL. MM. il re e la regina.* The word *san* (*santo*, etc.) is lower-cased when referring exclusively to a person: *san Francesco d'Assisi;* it is capitalized when abbreviated and when it is an integral part of the name of a place, a building, etc.: *S. Girolamo, Castel Sant'Angelo.*

6. *Personal pronouns.* The personal pronoun *io* is lower-cased, but the pronouns of formal address, *Ella, Lei, Loro* are capitalized.

7. *Church and state.* *La Chiesa,* when referring to the church as an institution, and *lo Stato,* when denoting the nation, are capitalized: *Consiglio di Stato.*

I. NORWEGIAN. *See* SCANDINAVIAN LANGUAGES.

J. PORTUGUESE

1. *Derivatives of proper names.* Derivatives of proper names are lower-cased unless used substantively: *os homens alemães* but *os Alemães.*

2. *Names of calendar divisions.* The names of the days of the week are lower-cased.

3. *Religious terms. Igreja* when referring to the church as an institution is capitalized.

4. *Titles of persons.* Names of positions, posts, or hierarchical dignitaries and words which designate titles are as a rule written with a small letter: *o arcebispo de Braja, o duque de Caxias, o presidente da Republica.* Exceptions include the use of capitals (1) to indicate special deference and (2) whenever the title follows a term of address. *Senhor Professor, Sr. Prof., Sua Excelencia o Presidente da Republica.*

5. *Personal pronouns.* The personal pronoun *eu* is lower-cased.

K. RUSSIAN

The capitalization of Russian is to follow the rules for the capitalization of English with the following exceptions and additions.

1. *Proper names.* Particles, prepositions and conjunctions forming part of a proper name are lower-cased, except when they are connected to the following part of the name by a hyphen.

фон Клаузевиц, ван Бетховен, Ван-Гог

2. *Derivatives of proper names.* Derivatives of proper names used with acquired independent meaning, or no longer identified with such names, are lower-cased. (Same as in English; repeated for examples.)

марксизм, марксистский, гегельянец

Names of peoples, races, and residents of specific localities are lower-cased.

араб, таджик, москвичи

3. *Names of regions, localities, and geographic features, including streets, parks, etc.* A common noun forming a part of a geographic name is lower-cased.

мыс Горн, остров Рудольфа, канал Москва-Волга

A common noun forming an integral part of a name is capitalized.

Кривой Рог, Белая Церковь, Богемский Лес

If the common noun is a foreign word which has not become a part of the Russian language, it is capitalized.

Рю-де-ла-Пе (рю—meaning street; Пе—meaning peace), Сыр-Дарья (дарья—meaning river)

117

The title or rank of the person in whose honor a place is named is lower-cased

остров королевы Виктории, мыс капитана Джеральда

Adjectives derived from names are lower-cased.

московские улицы

Geographic names applied to wines, species of animals, birds, etc., are lower-cased.

мадера, херес, сенбернар

4. *Names of countries and administrative divisions.* In commonly accepted names of groups of countries, the first word is capitalized.

Балканские страны

Non-official but commonly accepted names of countries, cities, and territorial divisions, are capitalized.

Советский Союз, Страна Советов, Приуралье, Белокаменная (for Moscow)

Administrative divisions of the USSR are capitalized as follows:

In the names of republics and autonomous republics every word is capitalized.

Башкирская Автономная Советская Социалистическая Республика

In the names of provinces, autonomous provinces, territories, regions, and village soviets, only the first word is capitalized.

Алма-Атинская область, Приморский край, Коми-Пермяцкий национальный округ, Егоршинский район, Краснинский сельсовет

In the names of the highest soviet and non-Russian governmental units and Communist party organizations, every word, except those in parentheses and the word "партия," is capitalized.

Верховный Совет СССР (also of the Union republics and autonomous republics), Совет Союза, Совет Национальностей, Всесоюзная Коммунистическая партия (большевиков). Рейхстаг, Конгресс США, Правительствующий Сенат

In other governmental units, only the first word and proper nouns are capitalized.

Государственная плановая комиссия СССР, Народный комиссариат иностранных дел, Военный совет Закавказского военного округа

Names of bureaus when used in the plural, and when used in a general sense, are lower-cased.

советы народных комиссаров, народный комиссариат

The word "Совет" is always capitalized in "Совет депутатов трудящихся."

Загорский районный Совет депутатов трудящихся

5. *Titles of persons.* Titles of the highest government officers are capitalized.

> Председатель Совета Народных Комиссаров, Маршал Советского Союза

6. *Names of organized bodies.* In the names of corporate bodies, only the first word and proper nouns are capitalized. If, however, part of the name is in quotation marks, only the first word within the quotes and proper nouns are capitalized.

> Академия наук СССР, Книжная палата, Профессиональный союз работников высшей школы и научных учреждений, Дом книги, завод "Фрезер," совхоз "Путь к социализму"

If the corporate body is also known by a part of its name the first word of the part is also capitalized.

> Государственный ордена Ленина академический Большой театр (Большой театр)

In the names of congresses, conferences, etc., the following words are not capitalized:

> съезд, конференция, сессия, пленум

The word "совет" when used to refer to the council of a society or institution is not capitalized.

7. *Names of historic events, etc.* In the names of historic periods and events, the first word, the distinctive word, and proper nouns are capitalized.

> Великая Октябрьская социалистическая революция, Возрождение, Третья республика, Парижская коммуна, Кровавое воскресенье, Ленский расстрел, Бородинский бой

Names of five-year plans are not capitalized.

> третья сталинская пятилетка, *but* соревнование имени Третьей Сталинской Пятилетки

Names of wars are capitalized.

> Франко-Прусская война, Русско-Японская война, Великая Отечественная война, Отечественная война

8. *Names of calendar divisions.* The names of calendar divisions are lower-cased.

> четверг, май

9. *Adverbs containing proper nouns.* Proper nouns that are parts of adverbs are lower-cased.

> по-пушкински

10. *Confessions of faith.* Confessions of faith and their adherents are lower-cased.

> католицизм, католик

L. SCANDINAVIAN

1. *Derivatives of proper names.* Adjectives derived from proper nouns a**
lower-cased.

2. *Names of organized bodies.* In the names of corporate bodies, generall
only the first word and the word following an adjective denoting royal privileg
are capitalized; other words, such as proper nouns, are governed by the othe
rules for capitalization.

3. *Names of calendar divisions.* Days of the week, months, and holidays a**
lower-cased.

4. *Titles of persons.* Titles are generally lower-cased.

5. *Personal pronouns.* In Danish, pronouns in the polite form are capitalize*
De, Dem, Deres; also the familiar form *I* (you) to distinguish it from *i* (in).

In Norwegian, the polite personal pronouns (direct address) *De, Dem, Dere*
Dykk, and *Dykkar* are capitalized.

In Swedish, the second-person pronouns, *Ni, Eder, Er,* are capitalized in corr*
spondence.

6. *Compound names.* In compound names, other than personal, only th
first word is generally capitalized: *Förenta staterna; Kronborg slott; Norske kirk*

M. SPANISH

1. *Derivatives of proper names.* Derivatives of proper names are lower-case*
Las mujeres colombianas.

Adjectives used substantively are lower-cased: *los franceses.*

2. *Names of calendar divisions.* The names of calendar divisions are lowe*
cased: *martes, otoño.*

3. *Religious terms. Iglesia* when referring to the church as an institution
capitalized.

4. *Titles of persons.* Titles of honor and address are capitalized only wh*
abbreviated: *senor (Sr.), doctor (Dr.), general (Gral.).*

Su Excelencia, Su Majestad, etc., are capitalized when used alone wheth
written out or abbreviated. When used with the name or another title they a
lower-cased: *su majestad el Rey.*

5. *Personal pronouns.* The personal pronoun *yo* is lower-cased; *Vd., Va*
(Ud., Uds.) are capitalized.

6. *Question within a sentence.* The first word of a question occurring within
sentence is usually lower-cased: *Cuando viene la noche ¿cómo se puede ver?*

N. SWEDISH. *See* SCANDINAVIAN LANGUAGES.

Appendix III. Abbreviations

Abbreviations are used except in the recording of titles (including alternative titles and subtitles), whether these are in the body of the entry, the series note list of contents, or cited elsewhere in the entry, and except in quoted notes. They need not be used if the brevity of the statement, or any other consideration, makes abbreviation in poor taste or if the resulting statement may not be clear. Single letter abbreviations are not used to begin a note.

The same abbreviation may be used for the corresponding word in another language if the abbreviation commonly used in that language has the same spelling. In case of doubt, abbreviation is not used.

The abbreviation may also be used for the last part of a compound word; e. g., Textausg. for Textausgabe.

A. GENERAL ABBREVIATIONS

Term	Abbreviation	Term	Abbreviation
Årgang	Årg.	bearbeitet	bearb.
Abteilung, Abtheilung	Abt., Abth.	Before Christ	B. C.
		bogtrykkeri	bogtr.
accompaniment	acc.	boktrykkeri	boktr.
afdeling	afd.	bövitett	böv.
alto	A [1]	Brother, -s	Bro.,[3] Bros.[3]
and	& [2]	Buchdrucker, Buchdruckerei	Buchdr.
Anno Domini	A. D.		
argraffiad	arg.	bulletin	bull.
arranged	arr.	capitolo	cap.
átdolgozott	átdolg.	centimeter	cm.
Auflage	Aufl.	circa	ca.
augmented	augm.	colored	col.
Ausgabe	Ausg.	Compagnia	Cia.
avdeling	avd.	Compagnie	Cie
Bändchen	Bdchn.	Company	Co.
Bände	Bde.	compare	cf.
Band (German)	Bd.	confer	cf.
band (Swedish)	bd.	Congress	Cong.
baritone	Bar.[1]	copyright	c
bass	B [1]	Corporation	Corp.

[1] Used only in supplementary notes to indicate voice range of vocal works.
[2] Used only in conventional titles for music.
[3] Used only in names of firms and other corporate bodies.

121

Term	Abbreviation	Term	Abbreviation
corrected	corr.	including	incl.
County	Co.	incorporated	inc.[2]
część	cz.	introduction	introd.
département	dép.	jaargang	jaarg.
department	dept.	Jahrgang	Jahrg.
diagram, -s	diagr., diagrs.	javitott	jav.
dissertation	diss.	Junior	Jr.
document	doc.	kiadás	kiad.
drukarnia	druk.	kötet	köt.
edition	ed.	księgarnia	księg.
édition	éd.	leaf, leaves	l.
engraved	engr.	Lieferung	Lfg.
enlarged	enl.	limited	ltd.[2]
establecimiento		livraison	livr.
tipográfico	estab. tip.	maatschappij	mij.
et alii	et al.	manuscript, -s	ms., mss.
facsimile, -s	facsim., facsims.	mezzosoprano	Mz.[1]
fascicle	fasc.	millimeter, -s	mm.
folded	fold.	miscellaneous	misc.
folio	fol.	nakład	nakł.
follow'g	ff.	nakładem	nakł.
frontispiece, -s	front., fronts.	neue Folge	n. F.
Gebrüder	Gebr.[2]	new series	new ser.
genealogical	geneal.	no date (of publi-	
government	govt.	cation)	n. d.
Government Print-		no place (of publi-	
ing Office	Govt. Print. Off.	cation)	n. p.
herausgegeben	hrsg.	nouveau, nouvelle	nouv.
Hermanos	Hnos.[2]	number, -s	no.
His (Her) Majes-		numbered	numb.
ty's Stationery		numer	nr.
Office	H. M. Stationery	numéro (French)	no
	Off.	numero (Italian)	n.
id est	i. e.	número (Spanish)	no.
illustration, -s	illus.	Nummer	Nr.
ilustración, -es	ilus.	nuovamente	nuov.
imienia	im.	oddział	oddz.
imprenta	impr.	översatt	övers.
imprimerie	impr.	omarbeidet	omarb.
Inaugural-Disser-		oplag	opl.
tation	Inaug.-Diss.	opplag	oppl.

[1] Used only in supplementary notes to indicate voice range of vocal works.
[2] Used only in names of firms and other corporate bodies.

ABBREVIATIONS

Term	Abbreviation
opracowane	oprac.
opus	op.
oversatt	overs.
page, -s	p.
part, -s	pt., pts.
parte	pt.
partie	ptie.
plate number	pl. no.
poprawione	popr.
portrait, -s	port., ports.
preface	pref.
préface	préf.
preliminary	prelim.
printing	print.
privately printed	priv. print.
pseudonym	pseud.
przejrzane	przejrz.
przerobione	przerob.
publishing	pub.
redakcja	red.
report	rept.
reviderade	revid.
revised	rev.
riveduto	riv.
rok	r.
rozszerzone	rozsz.
Senior	Sr.
série	sér.
series	ser.
session	sess.
signature	sig.
soprano	S [1]
stabilimento tipografico	stab. tip.
stronica	str.
supplement	suppl.
svazek	sv.
szám	sz.

Term	Abbreviation
szerkesztette	szerk.
talleres gráficos	tall. gráf.
Teil, Theil	T., Th.
tenor	T [1]
tipografía, tipográfica	tip.
title page	t. p.
tome	t.
tomo	t.
towarzystwo	tow.
typographical	typog.
typographie, typographique	typ.
udgave	udg.
udgivet	udg.
übersetzt	übers.
uitgaaf	uitg.
uitgegeven	uitg.
uitgevers	uitg.
umgearbeitet	umgearb.
unaccompanied	unacc.
Universitäts-Buchdrucker, Universitäts-Buchdruckerei	Univ.-Buchdr.
upplaga	uppl.
utarbeidet	utarb.
utgave	utg.
utgiven	utg.
various places	v. p.
verbesserte	verb.
vermehrte	verm.
versus	vs.
volume, -s	v., vol.,[4] vols.[4]
wydawnie	wyd.
wydawnictwo	wydawn.
wydział	wydz.
zeszyt	zesz.

[1] Used only in supplementary notes to indicate voice range of vocal works.
[4] Used at the beginning of a statement and before a roman numeral.

B. SLAVIC ABBREVIATIONS

Term	Abbreviation
видання	вид.
видавництво	вид-во
военный	воен.
всероссийский	всерос.
всесоюзный	всес.
вступление, вступительный	вступ.
выпуск	вып.
географический	геогр.
геологический	геол.
главный	глав.
год	г.
городской	гор.
государственный	гос.
губернский	губ.
державний	держ.
дополненный	доп.
друкарня	друк.
железнодорожный	жел-дор.
заглавие	загл.
и другие	и др.
и так далее	и т. д.
и тому подобное	и т. п.
издание	изд.
издательство	изд-во
имени	им.
Императорский	имп.
институт	ин-т
исправленный	испр.
исследовательский	иссл.
книга	кн.
книгоиздательство	кн-во
комитет	ком-т
литература	лит-ра
медицинский	мед.
народный	нар.
научный	науч.
областной	обл.
оборонный	обор.

Term	Abbreviation
обработанный	обраб.
общество	об-во
отделение	отд-ние
педагогический	педагог.
переработанный	перер.
пересмотренный	пересм.
полиграфический	полигр.
политический	полит.
предисловие	предисл.
промышленность	промышл.
редакция	ред.
сельскохозяйственный	селхоз
сокращенный	сокр.
социалистический	социалис.
социальный	соц.
страница	стр.
строительный	строит.
текстильный	текстил.
теоретический	теорет.
технический	техн.
типография	тип.
типо-литография	типо-лит.
товарищество	т-во
том	т.
транспортный	трансп.
украинский	укр.
университет, университетский	унив.
управление	упр.
учебный	учеб.
финансовый	фин.
химический	хим.
художественный	худож.
центральный	центр.
часть	ч.
экономический	экон.
электрический	электр.
энергетический	энерг.
юридический	юрид.

C. ABBREVIATIONS TO BE USED IN CITING BIBLIOGRAPHICAL SOURCES OF DATA

Any commonly used, self-explanatory abbreviations of the type listed below may be used in citing the source of data used in the catalog entry, so long as the use of abbreviations does not obscure the language of the source cited.

Term	Abbreviation	Term	Abbreviation
American	Amer.	directory	direct.
annuaire	ann.	encyclopedia	encycl.
annuario	ann.	English	Engl.
anuario	an.	history	hist.
bibliography	bibl.	Katalog	Kat.
biography	biog.	literature	lit.
British	Brit.	littérature	litt.
catalog, catalogue	cat.	museum	mus.
cyclopedia	cycl.	national	nat.
diccionnario	dicc.	report	rept.
dictionary	dict.		

D. ABBREVIATIONS OF THE NAMES OF STATES OF THE UNITED STATES, AND NAMES NOT ABBREVIATED

Ala.	Ill.	Minn.	N. C.	Tex.
Ariz.	Ind.	Miss.	N. D.	Utah
Ark.	Iowa	Mo.	Ohio	Vt.
Calif.	Kan.	Mont.	Okla.	Va.
Colo.	Ky.	Neb.	Or.	Wash.
Conn.	La.	Nev.	Pa.	W. Va.
Del.	Me.	N. H.	R. I.	Wis.
Fla.	Md.	N. J.	S. C.	Wyo.
Ga.	Mass.	N. M.	S. D.	
Idaho	Mich.	N. Y.	Tenn.	

E. ABBREVIATIONS OF OTHER PLACE NAMES

Name	Abbreviation	Name	Abbreviation
Alberta	Alta.	England	Eng.
British Columbia	B. C.	Germany	Ger.
Canada	Can.	Great Britain	Gt. Brit.
Cape Province	C. P.	Ireland	Ire.
District of Columbia	D. C.	New Brunswick	N. B.
Distrito Federal	D. F.	New Zealand	N. Z.

Name	Abbreviation	Name	Abbreviation
Nova Scotia	N. S.	Saskatchewan	Sask.
Ontario	Ont.	Scotland	Scot.
Prince Edward Island	P. E. I.	Territory of Hawaii	T. H.
Puerto Rico	P. R.	Union of Soviet Socialist	
Quebec	Que.	Republics	U. S. S. R.
Russian Socialist Federated		United States	U. S.
Soviet Republics	R.S.F.S.R.	Virgin Islands	V. I.

F. ABBREVIATIONS OF THE NAMES OF THE MONTHS

Bulgarian	Czech	Danish	Dutch	English	French
Ян.	led.	jan.	Jan.	Jan.	jan.
Фев.	ún.	febr.	Feb.	Feb.	fév.
Март	břez.	marts	Maart	Mar.	mars
Април	dub.	april	Apr.	Apr.	avril
Май	květ.	maj	Mei	May	mai
Юний	červ.	juni	Juni	June	juin
Юлий	červen.	juli	Juli	July	juil.
Авг.	srp	aug.	Aug.	Aug.	août
Септ.	září	sept.	Sept.	Sept.	sept.
Окт.	říj.	okt.	Oct.	Oct.	oct.
Ноем.	lis.	nov.	Nov.	Nov.	nov.
Дек.	pros.	dec.	Dec.	Dec.	déc.

German	Greek, Modern	Hungarian	Italian	Latvian	Norwegian
Jan.	'Ιαν.	jan.	genn.	jan.	jan.
Feb.	Φεβ.	feb.	febbr.	feb.	febr.
März	Μάρ.	márc.	mar.	màrts	mars
Apr.	'Απρ.	apr.	apr.	apr.	april
Mai	Μάϊος	máj.	magg.	maījs	mai
Juni	'Ιούν.	jun.	giugno	junijs	juni
Juli	'Ιούλ.	jul.	luglio	julijs	juli
Aug.	Αύγ.	aug.	ag.	aug.	aug.
Sept.	Σεπτ.	szept.	sett.	sept.	sept.
Okt.	'Οκτ.	oct.	ott.	okt.	okt.
Nov.	Νοέμ.	nov.	nov.	nov.	nov.
Dez.	Δεκ.	dec.	dic.	dec.	des.

126

ABBREVIATIONS

Polish	Portuguese	Rumanian	Russian	Serbo-Croatian	
stycz.	jan.	ian.	янв.	jaн.	siječ.
luty	fev.	feb.	февр.	фебр.	velj.
mar.	março	mar.	март	март	ožuj.
kwiec.	abril	apr.	апр.	април	trav.
maj.	maio	maiu	май	маj	svib.
czerw.	junho	junie	iюнь	jуни	lip.
lip.	julho	julie	iюль	jули	srp.
sierp.	agosto	aug.	авг.	ауг.	kol.
wrzes.	set.	sept.	сент.	септ.	ruj.
paźdz.	out.	oct.	окт.	окт.	list.
listop.	nov.	noem.	ноябрь	нов.	stud.
grudz.	dez.	dec.	дек.	дец.	pros.

Slovak	Slovenian	Spanish	Swedish	Ukrainian	Welsh
l'ad.	jan.	enero	jan.	січ.	Ion.
ún.	feb.	feb.	febr.	лют.	Chwe.
brez.	mar.	marzo	mars	бер.	Mawr.
dub.	apr.	abr.	april	квіт.	Ebr.
kvet.	maj	mayo	maj	трав.	Mai
červ.	jun.	jun.	juni	чер.	Meh.
červen.	jul.	jul.	juli	лип.	Gorf.
srp.	avg.	agosto	aug.	серп.	Awst
zári.	sept.	set.	sept.	вер.	Medi
ıuj.	okt.	oct.	okt.	жовт.	Hyd.
list.	nov.	nov.	nov.	лист.	Tach.
˙ .os.	dec.	dic.	dec.	груд.	Rhag.

Appendix IV. Numerals

A. ARABIC VS. ROMAN

Arabic numerals are substituted for roman except in the **recording of a title or** author statement, in the recording of pagination and references to pages, in citing quoted matter, and in the cataloging of incunabula.

> The second part of King Henry vi.
> By Jonathan Andrews, iii.
> xlii, 289 p.

If the substitution makes the statement less clear, as, for example, when roman and arabic numerals are used in conjunction to distinguish the volume, section, series, or other group, from the number, part, or other division of that group, the roman numerals are retained.

> (U. S. Dept. of State. Publication 3150. International organization and conference series, iii, 2)

B. ARABIC VS. NUMERALS SPELLED OUT

Arabic numerals are substituted for numerals that are spelled out if they occur elsewhere than in titles, in the names of corporate bodies, or in quoted matter.

> 4th ed.
> With 16 photographs by the author.

C. NUMERALS BEGINNING NOTES

If the first word of a note is a numeral it is spelled out if possible.

> First ed., published 1934, has title:
> Four no. a year, 1931; 5 no. a year, 1932–34.

D. NUMERALS BEGINNING TITLES. See 3:5 C.

E. ROMAN NUMERALS

Roman numerals are written in small capitals except those used in paging or page references and those appearing in lower case in the title or in a quoted note. Lower case numerals are used in paging or page references even though capitals appear in the work. The roman L (50) when standing alone is always printed with a small capital letter to distinguish it from the figure 1 (one).

F. INCLUSIVE NUMBERS

Inclusive numbers are given in full without mark of omission in the second number; e. g., p. 117–128. In inclusive dates within a century, except in titles, the century number is not repeated; e. g., 1828–64; if the century changed between the first and last dates, the full form is used; e. g., 1898–1902.

G. ORDINAL NUMERALS

For English works the ordinal numeral is indicated by the form 1st, 2d, 3d etc.; for foreign works: 1., 2., 3., etc.

Index

U. S. GOVERNMENT PRINTING OFFICE: 1949